Dinner On

Chef Jim Voltz

Ten complete, classic menus for simple but elegant meals perfect
for dinner with family and friends on the cottage porch

Printed in the United States of America

ISBN 978-1-60743-198-5

Illustrated by Chris Patterson
Design and Composition by Composure Graphics
Print Consulting by The Bishop Group

Thanks

So many of my close friends encouraged and supported me with this project and I want to thank them.

Most of the recipes in this book come from a collaboration of well-tested ideas of yours truly and recipes of my good friends, Kim Fairchild and Larry "Lars" Hilton.

All the wine suggestions are courtesy of another good friend of mine, Tim Richardson. Tim's wife, Jeri, provided her wonderful marinated roasted chicken recipe for Menu VIII.

Thanks to good friends, supporters, and advisors, Bob Weber and Betsie Hosick.

Also Nells Nelson of the East Shore Market and Sally Berlin of Crystal Crate and Cargo for their advice and support of my cooking classes.

Also thanks to Pris Rush for so scrupulously proofreading the draft.

Neighbor, friend, and artist, Chris Patterson, created all the illustrations. Her original sketch of our cottage that was used for the cover hangs in our entryway and has been enjoyed for years.

This cookbook and the lessons would never have been started or finished if it wasn't for Marjorie Elliott and her wonderful persuasive ways. Also my finest food critic and best friend, Nancy Myers.

Besides being good friends, all have been guests at my dinner parties and if you read the stories included with the recipes, you'll get to know a little bit more about these wonderful people and our dinners on the porch.

Thanks to all,

Jim Voltz

Contents

Introduction

The inspiration for this cookbook and the cooking classes given in July and August of 2008 is the result of the many summer dinner parties given on the porch of Sunny Shores Cottage on Crystal Lake near Frankfort, Michigan.

Sunny Shores is one of the smallest cottages on the Lake, about 800 square feet with a small galley kitchen and a 10 foot by 24 foot screened-in porch. The porch is nicknamed "The Gathering Place" and the name fits perfectly. Sit-down dinner parties for six to twelve guests are a weekly occurrence throughout the summer.

This book contains ten of my favorite menus to prepare for these dinner parties. Each one is a classic and elegant meal that is easy to prepare and always a hit with guests. Every menu has detailed recipes and instructions for preparing an appetizer, main course with side dishes, dessert, and the recommended wines to serve with the meal. Where I can, without affecting the quality, I've simplified the recipes. For example, using a good store-bought broth rather then making your own is fine here. The outcome will always be an elegant meal but casual enough for an enjoyable dinner with friends and family on the cottage porch.

All of these dinners have been prepared in my six-foot galley kitchen with a four burner, one oven, apartment-size stove. Lots of mise en place (put in place) and organization are required but all the menus in the book can be accomplished in this small kitchen. In fact, I consider mise en place to be one of the main secrets to successful cooking. Done properly, it ensures you have all the necessary ingredients and tools to successfully prepare a dish. It also makes cooking much more enjoyable. Mise en place is the simple task of getting all ingredients measured and set out along with the kitchen tools and pans you need to prepare a dish *before* you start cooking. Some of my other secrets for successful cooking and enjoyable entertaining are:

- Once you select your menu, *always* read every recipe in your menu plan several times before starting. This will ensure you are comfortable with the directions, understand the time needed for each dish, and have all the required utensils and pans.

- When a recipe calls for wine, *be sure* to use a quality wine like the ones recommended with each menu. If serving wine with the meal, use that same wine for cooking. Never, ever use a grocery store cooking wine. Always use a wine of a quality that you would drink.

- When using a major spice or herb in the main course meat, fish, or poultry dish, use the same spice or herb in the side dishes or appetizer to help coordinate the flavors. For example, this is evident in Menu X where the seasoned salt is used in both the meat and the vegetable.

- Don't overdo the menu. Limiting the menu to an appetizer, main course, one or two side dishes, and dessert is plenty. Too many items start to overwhelm flavors as well as guests. Keep it simple and elegant.

- Prepare as much as possible ahead of time, minimizing the last minute crunch on the afternoon of your dinner. If a dessert or sauce can be made a day ahead of time and kept in the refrigerator, do it. This makes the afternoon of your dinner party much less hectic, limiting mistakes, and giving you some wiggle room if something goes wrong.

- Clean-up as you go. This is contrary to what is often said but let's face it, the guests usually end up in the kitchen and it's nice if it's not a complete mess. It also helps me stay organized. In my kitchen, there's no dishwasher so clean-up must be continuous. I like to have as much preparation as possible done in advance and my kitchen looking like I haven't done anything to prepare for a party.

- Set your table and have all serving dishes organized early in the afternoon or even the day before.

- Fancy "tablescapes" are not necessary, in fact, I find them time consuming, expensive, and often too fussy. What I find works well for an elegant but casual look are a few small candles on the table, a pretty tablecloth or placemats, and un-ironed, cotton napkins. Please, no paper napkins! Pretty, not necessarily expensive, dishes and glassware finish off the table nicely.

- Finally, I like to leave the kitchen and sit down and rest at least 30 minutes before my guests arrive. That way I'm ready to enjoy the evening along with my guests.

A short story about some of the people who have come and shared our dinners on the porch accompanies each menu. In reading them, you will learn more about these wonderful people and our dinner parties. All the illustrations are actual drawings of Sunny Shores and other places in the area.

Use this cookbook when you want to prepare an elegant but casual dinner for your special friends and family to enjoy. I've had many successful dinners over the years using these recipes. So much so, my friends all encouraged me to develop cooking classes and write this cookbook.

Enjoy.

Nan Helps Prepare Dinner

I met Nancy Myers when I was five years old. She was the cute four-year-old girl in a red bathing suit in my swimming class.

Like me, Nan has been coming to Crystal Lake every summer of her life. Over 60 years ago our mothers dropped us off at the Congregational Assembly for swimming and tennis lessons and we've been friends ever since. This wonderful little cottage which we now share in the summer and where we have all the dinners on the porch, originally belonged to Nan's grandmother, Edith Wood. It was one of the original cottages on the lake and has been the base for many wonderful summers for the family for over 70 years.

When Nan and I are together, Nan is happy to let me do the cooking. Our friends assume she can't cook and Nan doesn't say anything to make them think differently. But her naughty little secret is starting to come out. As the summers go by and we have more dinner parties, more people witness Nan expertly helping me in the kitchen. Many of our friends are starting to suspect that Nan knows how to cook–and she does. She just doesn't like to do it very often. Her sister, Shirley, describes Nan as someone who can cook gourmet but can't cook "everyday".

Menu I is one of Nan's favorite meals. She always requests it for her birthday dinner.

Nan's Menu
(6 to 8 servings)

**Avocado stuffed with Crabmeat
or Tiny Shrimp with Remoulade Sauce
on a Bed of Baby Greens**

**Roasted Rock Cornish Game Hens
with Lemon and Rosemary**

Baked Zucchini stuffed with Couscous

Lemon tart with Raspberry Coulis

This is a great menu to prepare for a dinner party of six to eight which can be done very elegantly or porch casual. The only really last minute item is peeling the avocado so it won't blacken. The tart and coulis can and should be done a day in advance. The zucchini can be done a day in advance or a few hours ahead and reheated while the hens are resting after roasting.

Appetizer

Avocados, 5 to 8, ripe but not squishy

Lump Crabmeat, 1 pound, not canned, (this can be found at Sam's Club) *or* Tiny Shrimp, 1 pound, cooked and shelled (frozen is ok)

Mixed Baby greens, 1 bag, enough to just cover individual serving plates

Remoulade Sauce

Mayonnaise	Egg
Cornichons	Capers
Parsley	Tarragon
Dijon Mustard	Garlic
Lemons, 2	

Main Course

Rock Cornish Game Hens, 6 to 8, they usually come in packages of 2 in the freezer section of your market. Rarely do you find them fresh, frozen is ok.

Fresh rosemary, 1 package from your local store's produce section or from your herb garden

Lemons, 4, try to get seedless Meyer lemons.

Zucchini, 3 to 4 medium size ($\frac{1}{2}$ lengthwise per person)

Unsalted Butter, 3 sticks ($\frac{3}{4}$ pound)

Yellow Onion, 1 medium size

Couscous, 1 box of quick cooking couscous

Garlic, 2 cloves

Chicken Stock, 1 can low sodium chicken stock

Dried currants or raisins

Cinnamon, ground

Pine Nuts

Dessert

Pre-made shortbread crust from your grocer, one 9 inch crust, usually found in the baking aisle (not frozen)

Unsalted Butter, 1 stick ($\frac{1}{4}$ pound)

Eggs, 8 large size (this is a total of nine eggs for the entire menu)

Frozen raspberries, one 12-oz package

Lemons, 4 (This is a total of 10 fresh lemons for the entire menu)

Remoulade
(can be made in advance)

1. Put one cup of good mayonnaise in a medium size mixing bowl

2. Stir in:

    1 hard boiled egg, minced

    1 Tbls minced Cornichons

    1 Tbls drained minced capers

    1 Tbls chopped fresh parsley

    $1\frac{1}{2}$ tsp chopped fresh tarragon

    1 small minced garlic clove

    $\frac{1}{2}$ tsp Dijon mustard

    Salt and pepper to taste
    (recommend $\frac{1}{2}$ tsp salt and $\frac{1}{4}$ tsp freshly ground pepper)

3. Refrigerate until ready for use

Crabmeat (or shrimp) Stuffed Avocados

1. Check crabmeat (or shrimp) for any shells

2. Cut avocados in half, lengthwise, remove seed and then scoop out flesh with large spoon in one piece.Squeeze fresh lemon juice all over lightly

3. Place small amount of greens on each individual serving plate

4. Place one avocado half on each plate in the center of the greens

5. Fill avocado half with crabmeat or shrimp (heaping)

6. Top crabmeat (shrimp) with 2 Tbls remoulade sauce

7. Put a lemon wedge on each plate and serve with extra remoulade on the side

Baked Zucchini

1. Preheat oven to 400 degrees Fahrenheit

2. Lightly oil baking dish large enough to handle
   6 to 8 zucchini halves

3. Wash and trim stems of zucchini. Cut zucchini in half lengthwise.
   Sprinkle lightly with salt and pepper. Place cut side down in baking
   pan and roast for 10 to 12 minutes. Cut side should be lightly
   browned.

4. Remove from oven and let cool until you can pick-up and handle
   comfortably. Using a teaspoon, scoop out the centers of the
   zucchini creating a boat shell.

5. Finely chop the removed zucchini pulp and set aside

6. Heat a large non-stick skillet over medium heat

   a. Add 2 Tbls extra-virgin olive oil and $\frac{1}{2}$ cup finely chopped
      onions, cook 5 minutes

   b. Add all the zucchini pulp finely chopped, $\frac{2}{3}$ cup uncooked
      couscous, and 2 cloves minced garlic. Stir until coated
      with the oil

   c. Add $1\frac{1}{2}$ cups low sodium chicken stock, 2 Tbls dried
      currants or raisins, and 1 tsp ground cinnamon

   d. Bring to a boil, cover and cook over low heat for 5 minutes

   e. Uncover and let cool to room temperature

   f. Stir in 2 Tbls roasted pine nuts

7. Spoon couscous mixture into zucchini boats
   (mound as much as possible)

8. Arrange in baking pan and cover with foil, bake at 350 degrees
   Fahrenheit for 20 minutes – *or* - refrigerate overnight. If you
   refrigerate overnight, take it out of the refrigerator 3 hours
   before serving and then bake at 350 degrees Fahrenheit for
   20 to 30 minutes after removing hens from oven.
   (Hens should rest this long before serving)

Rock Cornish Game Hens

1. Thaw in refrigerator 2 days before cooking, following directions on package

2. Preheat oven to 350 degrees Fahrenheit

3. Rinse hens in cold water and pat dry

4. Squeeze lemon juice all over and inside hens then liberally salt and pepper both the hen cavity and skin

5. Put lemon pieces from squeezing and bruised rosemary sprigs inside hen cavity. (bruise rosemary by placing sprigs on chopping board and hitting with the back of a large knife)

6. Place hens on rack in shallow roasting pan (use 2 pans if necessary so hens do not touch each other)

7. Place hens in oven and roast for 15 minutes. Baste liberally with melted butter. Bake another 15 minutes and baste again. Bake another 15 minutes and baste again. Bake final 15 minutes (total of one hour) and remove from oven.

8. Cover hens with foil and let sit for 20 or 30 minutes. (Now put zucchini boats in oven for 20 to 30 minutes)

Serving: Place one hen and one zucchini boat on each plate and serve. Don't forget to put a small empty plate at each place for bones.

Lemon Tart

1. Bake shortbread crust as directed on package using egg wash. Let cool

2. Preheat oven to 350 degrees Fahrenheit

3. Separate 8 large egg yolks
   (reserve whites for another use, if desired)

4. Squeeze and strain enough lemons for $\frac{1}{2}$ cup juice

5. Grate enough lemon zest for 1 Tbls

6. Combine in heat proof bowl or double boiler 1 cup of sugar and 8 Tbls (1 stick) unsalted butter cut into small pieces.

7. Put the bowl into pan with 1 inch water or over double boiler and stir until butter is melted into sugar over low heat.

8. Remove the bowl from heat and beat in the egg yolks with whisk until no yellow streaks remain.

9. Stir in $\frac{1}{2}$ cup fresh lemon juice.

10. Return bowl to pan or double boiler, and, stirring gently, heat on med/low heat until thickened (lightly coats the back of a spoon), about 8 minutes.

11. Stir in the 1 Tbls lemon zest

12. Pour mixture into tart crust and bake for about 15 to 20 minutes or until center looks set but still very quivery

13. Let cool completely on a cooling rack

14. Lightly oil or butter a piece of plastic wrap and press directly onto the filling and refrigerate overnight

Serving: Let warm to room temperature. Take a heavy duty scissors and cut aluminum pie tin to remove. This enables serving without breaking crust and entire tart can be put on a beautiful serving platter. Place individual slices on plates and using squeeze bottle, crisscross tart and plate with coulis or decorate as desired.

Raspberry Coulis

NOTES

1. Thaw one 12-oz package raspberries

2. Push raspberries through a fine strainer using a flexible rubber spatula. This takes some time and effort but is well worth it. Do it in batches and discard seeds after each batch.

3. Put raspberry pulp in blender or food processor. Add:
   a. 3 Tbls sugar
   b. 1 Tbls fresh lemon juice
   c. Puree until smooth

4. Strain again through sieve. Taste and add a little more sugar or lemon juice as desired

5. Cover and refrigerate overnight until ready to serve

Wine

Tim suggests: Gigondas (French, from the Rhone valley).

Alternatives: Cotes-du-Rhone, Chateauneuf-du-Pape, American Syrah

Pete and Amy Open the Crystal View Café

Pete and Amy Taylor are long-time Crystal Lake summer residents. During the winter, they live in Tampa, Florida where Amy teaches ballet and Pete owns a comic book and guitar store. In 2007, they agreed to take over management of the small, summer, beachside restaurant on Crystal Lake, The Crystal View Café. The Crystal View has been in operation for years, I even went there as a child when it was known as the Polka Dot Café. When Pete and Amy took over, they cleaned up the interior of the cafe, but most importantly, they upgraded the menu. They asked for my help over the winter to develop a short order menu that would appeal to adults as well as kids. In addition to hamburgers and hot dogs, there are now items on the menu such as grilled Chicken Dijon and veggie wraps. After many very long days and lots of hard work, Pete and Amy opened the revamped cafe for business in early June. To help celebrate their opening day and give them a much-needed break, I invited them to dinner on the porch that evening. They came even though they were exhausted but they didn't make it to dessert. Amy fell asleep on the day-bed in the corner of the porch and Pete decided it was time for them to go home.

Following is the menu for that evening, including the dessert that Pete and Amy missed.

Opening Night Menu
(6 servings)

Texas Shrimp

Grilled Lake Trout

Braised Cabbage and Leeks

Yogurt Cake

Lake Trout, in my opinion, is the best clear water fish in Michigan. It is stronger in flavor then white fish but not as strong as salmon. This recipe calls for grilling using a flipable grill, it is very hard to turn fish over with a spatula. The Texas Shrimp is a great spicy starter and the yogurt cake is a light and fresh citrus finish.

Shopping List

Appetizer

30 large, pre-cooked and shelled shrimp

1 small bunch each fresh parsley, cilantro, and green onions

2 limes

3 cloves garlic

1 medium tomato

1 medium yellow onion

Catsup

Hot sauce (your choice or Tabasco)

Olive Oil

1 head of lettuce of your choice

Main Course

3 filets (approx. 3 lbs total) fresh lake trout

3 lemons

1 bunch each fresh thyme, oregano, parsley (or dried "herbes de provence")

1 large green cabbage

2 leeks

4 ounces low sodium chicken broth

Celery Salt

Dessert

½ cup plain yogurt

2 large eggs

1 cup sugar

1½ cups flour

1 tsp baking soda

1 Tbls safflower oil

Orange juice (2 oranges fresh squeezed or not from concentrate orange juice)

Confectioners Sugar (for dusting)

¼ tsp vanilla extract

Texas Shrimp

1. Finely dice the following and put in a bowl
   a. Onion (one medium)
   b. Tomato with juices
   c. 3 cloves garlic
   d. Parsley
   e. Cilantro
   f. Green onions

2. Add and mix:
   a. Juice from the limes
   b. 1 Tbls Olive oil
   c. 1 Tbls Catsup
   d. $\frac{1}{2}$ tsp hot sauce

3. Put shrimp in plastic bag and pour mixture over top. Lightly message to cover shrimp and refrigerate for at least 1 hour, but not over 4 hours.

Serving: Put lettuce leaves or shredded lettuce on small plates and arrange 5 shrimp on each plate with a small amount of the marinade on top.

NOTES

Braised Cabbage and Leeks

Prepare the cabbage and leeks first and keep warm on stove or in the oven, or, this can be made ahead and reheated.

1. Cut cabbage into quarters and remove hard core

2. Slice quarters across in $\frac{1}{4}$ inch slices

3. Cut bottom and most of green part off of leeks

4. Slice leeks across in $\frac{1}{4}$ inch slices

5. Rinse leeks in colander and drain if any dirt is spotted

6. Put on paper towels or large dish towel and pat dry

7. Heat large skillet or wok on medium heat

8. Add 2 Tbls Olive oil

9. Add cabbage and leeks and sauté for approximately 5 to 8 minutes until lightly sauted and wilted.

10. Add 1 tsp celery salt and $\frac{1}{2}$ tsp black pepper and stir

11. Add 4 oz chicken broth, stir and reduce heat to simmer

12. Simmer for about 10 to 15 minutes, stirring frequently, adding more chicken broth to keep moist

13. Cover and keep warm until ready to serve

Lake Trout

NOTES

1. Get grill ready, charcoal or gas, and use medium high, direct heat. Put flip grill on top of the charcoal or gas grill to heat.

2. Check filets for any pin bones and remove if necessary with needle nose pliers or tweezers. Also, cut off any white fatty areas.

3. Place filets on large tray

4. Squeeze 1 to 2 lemons over fish (depending on size and juices of lemons) making sure no seeds remain on fish.

5. Dice fresh herbs (thyme, oregano, and parsley) finely and sprinkle over fish or use dried "herb de Provence."

6. Sprinkle with 1 tsp salt and fresh ground black pepper to taste.

7. Take flip grill off grill and place filets inside.

8 Grill, flesh side down for 3 to 5 minutes depending on the thickness — do not overcook

9. Flip and grill, skin side down, for 3 to 5 minutes until skin is charring and flesh is resilient to touch.

10. Remove from grill, open flip grill and using 2 spatulas, remove fish from skin onto clean tray or serving platter.

Note: Put flip grill back on fire to burn skin off rack and get fish smell from grill

Serving: Serve family style with seedless wedges of lemon

Yogurt Cake

You will need a 9-inch round or square, deep cake pan for this recipe. It does not do well in two shallow pans and then stacked.

1. Preheat oven to 350 degrees Fahrenheit

2. Grease a 9 inch round or square, deep cake pan with butter

3. Put the following into a large mixing bowl:
   a. $\frac{1}{2}$ cup plain yogurt
   b. 1 cup sugar
   c. $1\frac{1}{2}$ cups flour
   d. 2 large eggs
   e. 1 Tbls Safflower oil
   f. 1 tsp baking soda
   g. $\frac{1}{8}$ tsp salt
   h. $\frac{1}{4}$ cup fresh orange juice
   i. $\frac{1}{4}$ tsp pure vanilla extract

4. Mix well by stirring with a wire whisk

5. Pour into greased cake pan and lightly drop on table to release any air bubbles from the batter.

6. Bake for 15 to 20 minutes until a toothpick inserted in center comes out clean

7. Remove from oven, prick a few holes in the top with a fork and pour $\frac{1}{4}$ cup fresh orange juice over cake

8. Let cool for 10 minutes and turn out onto a wire rack to cool.

Serving: Lightly dust the cake with confectioners sugar sifted through a strainer and serve at room temperature

Wine

Tim Suggests: Austrian Riesling or Alsace Pinot Blanc

Alternatives: There are nice Michigan counterparts, ask your local wine store owner.

NOTES

Kim Introduces Marjorie To The Group

Kim Fairchild is a very good cook and one of my oldest friends. We've spent many wonderful summers cooking together, testing new recipes and perfecting the old ones. Last summer Kim brought a longtime friend of his, Marjorie Elliott, over to meet the crowd and have dinner with us on the porch. Marjorie had recently retired and was looking forward to spending the entire summer at Crystal Lake as she did when she was a child. When I asked her if she cooked, she replied, "Let me give you an example of one of the dishes I'm known for, strawberry shortcake. You take fresh or frozen strawberries, put them on top of a Twinkie, and cover the whole thing with whipped cream out of a pressurized can." I became good friends with Marjorie anyway.

I even "made" Marjorie's Strawberry Shortcake for one of our dinners on the porch and, needless to say, it created much conversation and more then a little laughter. But everyone readily ate and enjoyed it, with one exception, our next door neighbor. She pronounced it inedible without trying it, creating more laughter and a few jeers from the other guests.

Following are the recipes for the dinner I served that night, including Marjorie's Strawberry Shortcake.

Menu III

Neighborly Chicken Menu
(6 servings)

Asian Coleslaw

Paillard of Chicken

French Fries

Marjorie's Strawberry Shortcake

The Asian coleslaw can be served as an appetizer but it would really go well accompanying the main course. You can substitute beef or pork for the chicken and cook as directed. The French fries are from an original "Cordon Bleu" recipe and are the best. I fixed them twice at Sunny Shores last summer and guests were standing around the stove eating them as they were prepared. Nothing could top the meal better then Marjorie Elliott's special strawberry shortcake dessert.

Shopping List

Appetizer

1 small red cabbage

1 large green cabbage

1 tart green apple

1 bunch green onions

Vinaigrette

$\frac{1}{4}$ cup rice vinegar

3 Tbls olive oil

2 Tbls chopped cilantro

2 Tbls grated ginger (You can get fresh grated ginger in a plastic tube in the fresh herb section of your grocery store.)

1 Tbls soy sauce

$\frac{1}{4}$ tsp celery salt

$\frac{1}{4}$ tsp crushed red pepper

Main Course

6 boneless, skinless chicken breast halves

$\frac{1}{2}$ cup all-purpose flour

1 tsp onion powder

8 Tbls (1 stick) butter

3 Tbls olive oil

2 lemons

1 small jar capers

8 large baking potatoes

1 small bunch parsley

Oil for frying

Dessert

6 Twinkies (yes, Hostess Twinkies)

2 quarts fresh strawberries

1 can pressurized whipped cream

Asian Coleslaw
(prepare ahead 1 day or at least 3 hours)

1. Finely chop the red and green cabbage and put in large bowl

2. Slice the green onions (approximately $\frac{1}{4}$ inch) and add to cabbage

3. Do not dice or peel the apple until you are ready to toss with the vinaigrette (It turns brown quickly without the vinaigrette)

4. For the vinaigrette, mix together the following and then pour over the cabbage mixture, then add the diced apple and toss:

    a) $\frac{1}{4}$ cup rice vinegar

    b) 3 Tbls olive oil

    c) 2 Tbls freshly chopped cilantro

    d) 2 Tbls grated ginger (you can get fresh grated ginger in a plastic tube in the fresh herb section of your grocery store)

    e) 1 Tbls soy sauce

    f) $\frac{1}{4}$ tsp celery salt

    g) $\frac{1}{4}$ tsp crushed red pepper

    h) $\frac{1}{4}$ tsp salt

    i) $\frac{1}{4}$ tsp pepper

Cover and chill until ready to serve

Paillard of Chicken
(this basically means flattened and quickly sautéed)

1. Put each chicken breast between 2 pieces of plastic wrap and pound evenly with a smooth-faced mallet or flat-bottomed heavy pan to about $\frac{1}{4}$ inch thickness all over.

2. Very lightly salt and pepper both sides

3. Mix together $\frac{1}{2}$ cup all-purpose flour, 1 tsp salt, and 1 tsp onion powder and put the mixture in a low-sided pan.

4. Very lightly dredge each chicken breast, both sides, in the flour mixture and set aside

5. Squeeze lemons and set aside

6. Drain capers and set aside

7. Heat a large skillet on medium/high heat (you will probably have to cook the paillard in 2 to 3 batches depending on the size of the chicken breasts and the size of the skillet) and melt 2 Tbls butter and 1 Tbls olive oil for each batch.

8. Saute each breast for approximately 2 to 3 minutes or until golden brown on each side. Put on plate and keep warm until all are sautéed

9. Reduce heat to medium and add lemon juice and capers to pan with 2 Tbls butter

10. Place each paillard back into pan just to coat each side and place on serving platter

11. Pour remaining juice and capers from pan over the paillards, sprinkle with chopped parsley and serve

I would suggest doing steps 7 through 11 after the French fries are prepared, but you could keep the chicken warm in a very low oven. *Do not overcook!*

French Fries

1. Peel potatoes

2. Cut into long $\frac{1}{4}$ by $\frac{1}{4}$ inch sticks, as close to the same size as possible for even cooking

3. Place sticks into large bowl of salted *ice* water for 1 hour

4. If using a deep fryer, preheat to 375 degrees Fahrenheit. If using a deep skillet on the stove top, preheat oil to medium/high

5. Drain potato sticks between very absorbent kitchen or bath towels, blotting out as much water as possible

6. Cook sticks in small batches (cooking in small batches is one of the secrets) and remove them just as they start to brown (another secret, don't brown at this time)

7. Place batches on newspaper (not paper towels, this is another secret) to drain and cool

8. Continue until all potato sticks are semi-cooked

9. Increase heat to 425 degrees Fahrenheit or high on stove

10. Again, in small batches, fry semi-cooked sticks until golden brown. (This should be a very fast process). This time it is ok to drain on paper towels and salt as desired

11. Keep the batches warm in oven until all sticks are fried.

Serving: Serve as soon as possible (if there are any left from the kitchen help) with ketchup (U.S.) mustard or vinegar (European) or mayonnaise (Canadian). Again, I would have the fries all done and kept warm before final preparation of the paillard.

NOTES

Marjorie's Strawberry Shortcake

1. Clean and slice 2 quarts of fresh strawberries (frozen may be used if you want to make this even easier)

2. Place in large bowl and add $\frac{1}{4}$ cup sugar. (Amount of sugar depends on the sweetness of the berries and your preference on the level of sweetness. If they are good, homegrown berries, I usually do not add any sugar). Set aside

3. Slice each Twinkie into $\frac{1}{2}$ inch thick slices and arrange on individual serving plates

4. Spoon strawberries over Twinkies

5. Top with whipped cream from a can and serve

Wine

Tim suggests: Chianti

Alternatives: other North Italian reds (e.g. Barbera, Valpolicella), red Saumur or Chinon (French), Beaujolais (e.g. Brouilly). American table wine

Local possibility: Michigan Cabernet Franc

NOTES

Lars Has Rehearsals and Misses Dinner but Leaves Dessert

Larry "Lars" Hilton is one of my close friends and a regular guest at our dinners on the porch. He also happens to be a good cook, and over the years, has become a particularly good pastry chef. But he also sings and sometimes the two hobbies conflict. Last summer, Lars played Earthquake McGoon in a local production of "Lil' Abner." Rehearsals for the play were not going well and the cast was staying well past dinnertime to work out the problems. We were all sorry when Lars called and said he was not going to make it for dinner, especially since he was supposed to bring dessert. Well, Lars came through with the makings for a wonderful Cherry Cobbler, dropped it off, and went back to rehearsals. We enjoyed it immensely. I only wish we had tried a little harder to save Lars a piece.

I should also mention that everything worked out, the play went off without a hitch, and several of us went to see it on opening night. Menu 4 is the dinner Lars missed, including his wonderful Cherry Cobbler.

Star Studded Menu
(8 servings)

Cucumber Salad with Mint

Butterflied Grilled Leg of Lamb

Roasted Asparagus

Brown Rice

Cherry Cobbler

Leg of Lamb on the grill makes a statement on its own and having it butterflied makes it cook in about the same time as a thick steak. If given time, your butcher will butterfly it for you or you can carefully do it yourself. Serving the cucumber salad with mint before or with the lamb is a perfect combination. Roasting fresh local Michigan asparagus gives it a deeper, richer flavor that you can't get by steaming. Fresh local red cherries in a warm cobbler make a fitting end to this great dinner on the porch.

Shopping List

Appetizer

3 large English cucumbers

8-oz plain yogurt

12 large fresh mint leaves

1 to 2 garlic cloves

Butter lettuce leaves (if used as an appetizer)

Main Course

1, 6-pound butterflied leg of lamb

2 heads garlic

4 to 6 sprigs fresh rosemary

2 to 3 lbs fresh asparagus (6 to 8 spears per person)

12-oz brown rice

24-oz low sodium beef broth

1 Tbls butter

1 loaf good crusty bread, if desired

Dessert

3 cups sour red cherries

1 cup sugar (for fruit)

1 Tbls sugar (for shortcake topping)

1 cup flour

$\frac{1}{2}$ tsp baking powder

$\frac{1}{2}$ cup milk

1 Tbls corn starch

3 Tbls butter

$\frac{1}{2}$ tsp cinnamon

Cucumber Salad with Mint
(can be served as an appetizer or with the main
course as a condiment)

1. Peel and slice the cucumbers thinly (approx. $\frac{1}{8}$ inch thick)

2. Put slices into a large colander and sprinkle with salt

3. Let the cucumber slices drain for at least 30 minutes

4. Stir together in medium size bowl:
   a. 8-oz plain yogurt
   b. 1 tsp salt
   c. $\frac{1}{2}$ tsp fresh cracked black pepper
   d. 1 tsp minced garlic

5. Stack the 12 mint leaves one on top of the other, roll them up like a cylinder and slice crosswise into thin slices. Add mint to dressing.

6. Wrap the cucumber slices (without rinsing) in a clean dish towel and gently squeeze to dry them. Add to mint sauce and toss at least 1 hour before serving. This can also be done up to 6 hours before serving and the salad kept in the refrigerator. Do not prepare a day in advance as the cucumber will weep and make the mint sauce watery.

Serving: As an appetizer, serve on butter lettuce leaves. As a condiment, serve in a bowl family style with the main course.

Grilled Butterflied Lamb

NOTES

It will take about 30 minutes to grill a 6 lb, 3 inch thick piece of lamb on a hot indirect grill fire. This is for medium rare lamb. The following should be done at least 2 hours in advance and left at room temperature or prepared 1 day in advance and refrigerated overnight. Bring to room temperature before grilling.

1. Lay the lamb on a large baking sheet

2. Slice 4 large garlic cloves into thin slices

3. Put 4 to 6 sprigs of rosemary on a cutting board and bruise with the back of a large knife or a heavy pan.

4. Cut small slits on surface of lamb and insert garlic slices. (It's easiest to make a slit and insert garlic before you remove your paring knife.)

5. Salt and Pepper the top of the lamb according to taste. (At least 1 Tbls salt and 2 tsp pepper)

6. Spread bruised rosemary over lamb

7. Lightly sprinkle lamb with olive oil (about 2 Tbls)

8. Grill on indirect heat

Roasted Asparagus

1. Preheat oven to 400 degrees Fahrenheit

2. Rinse asparagus under running water and place on paper towels to drain. Michigan asparagus does not need to be trimmed before cooking.

3. Place asparagus in large roasting pan so that most pieces lie flat, some overlap is ok

4. Sprinkle with olive oil, about 2 Tbls, and mix to coat all sides.

5. Sprinkle with salt and freshly ground black pepper (about 1 Tbls salt and 1 tsp pepper)

6. Top with 2 Tbls of minced garlic and toss

You can prepare the dish to this point 4 or 5 hours in advance and let it stand at room temperature.

7. Roast for 15 to 20 minutes and serve warm or at room temperature.

Brown Rice

Typically, 1 cup of dry rice will serve 6 people. If you have good eaters or want some left over, use $1\frac{1}{2}$ cups of rice for this recipe.

1. In a large sauce pan with lid, over medium heat, place 1 Tbls butter and 1 Tbls olive oil

2. Add rice and sauté for 2 minutes, stirring frequently.

3. Add 3 cups low sodium beef stock and stir.

4. Bring to a low boil.

5. Lower heat, cover and simmer for 40 minutes.

6. Remove cover and cook another 5 minutes, stirring frequently to remove any excess liquid. This makes a creamy, almost risotto type rice.

Note: Basic cooking time for the 3 main course items:

1. Lamb—30 minutes plus 15 minutes of resting time

2. Asparagus—15 minutes

3. Rice—45 minutes

Serving: Allow lamb to rest 15 minutes before slicing thinly across the bias and place on large platter. Pile asparagus on large platter and place rice in a bowl. Serve family style, it looks really sumptuous on the porch table. A nice crusty bread and butter would make a good addition.

Cherry Cobbler

A classic Michigan dessert using fresh red cherries from the Cherry Capital of the world, Traverse City, Michigan. You can substitute almost any fresh fruit such as peaches, blueberries or strawberries by varying the amount of sugar, depending on the sweetness of the fruit. This is a quick, easy dessert which is best served warm.

Shortcake For Topping:

1. Mix well using a wire whisk:

    a. 1 cup flour

    b. 1 Tbls sugar

    c. $1\frac{1}{2}$ tsp baking powder

    d. $\frac{1}{2}$ tsp salt

2. Cut in with pastry blender or use fingers, 3 Tbls hard butter (not frozen, just from the refrigerator)

3. Stir in $\frac{1}{2}$ cup milk to make soft dough, set aside (this can be made a few hours in advance and covered with a damp towel)

Fruit Cobbler Base: Preheat oven to 400 degrees Fahrenheit

1. In a medium sauce pan add:

    a. 1 cup sugar for cherries

    b. 1 Tbls corn starch

    c. 1 cup warm water

2. Bring to a boil, stirring to dissolve sugar

3. Add 3 cups pitted cherries and stir

4. Pour mixture into 2-quart, greased baking dish (approximately 8x8x2 or 10x6x2)

5. Sprinkle with $\frac{1}{2}$ tsp cinnamon

6. Drop shortcake by spoonfuls on top of fruit

7. Lightly dot with butter

8. Bake for 30 minutes

Serving: Serve in bowls with ice cream, whipping cream, or just heavy cream

Wine

Tim suggests: A good full-bodied Bordeaux or American Claret

Alternatives: A good Cabernet Sauvignon would also go nicely with lamb.

Jim Cooks for Forty on Guest Chef Night

The Crystal View Café started having a "Guest Chef" night in July of 2007. Pete and Amy Taylor had first proposed this to me during the previous winter at their home in Tampa, Florida. We liked the idea but knew that preparing full dinners was going to be a challenge. The Crystal View only has a grill, no burners and no oven. I agreed to be the first "guinea pig" and prepare the menu that follows with the help of Kim Fairchild and Larry "Lars" Hilton. The estimated reservations were for 30 but ended up at 40 with a wait list. Now enters the challenge, preparing Coq au Vin for 40 in my small galley kitchen with a four burner, one oven, apartment-size stove and then transporting it to the Cafe. Browning 40 chicken legs and 40 thighs using two medium skillets takes a lot of time and patience. Making the braising sauce and getting eighty pieces of chicken into two casseroles when only one will fit into the oven at a time was a huge challenge. In spite of the limited kitchen, everything went well and the dinner was a great success and was followed by three more "Guest Chef" nights.

Menu V

Guest Chef Menu
(6 to 8 servings)

Tomato Blue Cheese Tart

Coq au Vin with Egg Noodles

Crème Brulee

Originally in France, Coq Au Vin was really called a French country fricassée and included all the parts of an old rooster. The dish has been upgraded and usually consists of legs and thighs only, as the breast is better suited for poaching or lighter cooking. Since there are really no vegetable side dishes, the tomato blue cheese tart is a great starter, and, no one can resist dessert if it's crème brulee.

shopping List

Appetizer

4 semi-ripe (not squishy) roma tomatoes

8-oz Blue Cheese

2 Tbls heavy cream

1 Tbls fresh thyme or 1 tsp dried

3 flat anchovy fillets

1 cup all-purpose flour

$\frac{1}{2}$ stick butter

1 tsp olive oil

Main Course

8 chicken legs and 8 chicken thighs

4 slices thick-cut bacon

2 large yellow onions

2 carrots

4 Tbls unsalted butter

1 bottle red wine (we suggest a Shiraz or Merlot)

16-oz chicken stock (low sodium preferred)

2 heapingTbls tomato paste

4 Bay Leaves

2 heaping tsp fresh thyme or 1 tsp dried

2 heaping tsp fresh oregano or 1 tsp dried

1 package frozen pearl onions

16-oz button or thick sliced larger mushrooms

Fresh parsley for garnish

1 large package egg noodles

2 heaping Tbls all-purpose flour

Dessert

16-oz heavy cream

8 eggs

Pure vanilla extract

$\frac{1}{2}$ cup sugar

Sugar for caramelizing

Tomato, Blue Cheese Tart

Pastry:

1. Use a 9 inch tart pan. Preheat oven to 350 degrees Fahrenheit
2. Put 1 cup all purpose flour and a pinch of salt into a food processor*
3. Add $\frac{1}{2}$ stick frozen butter sliced into $\frac{1}{4}$ inch pieces
4. Pulse until butter is covered with flour but still in pieces
5. Slowly add 3 to 5 Tbls *ice* water while pulsing until a ball is formed. Do not over mix.
6. At this point you can either break up the dough ball into little pieces and hand press into the torte pan *or* knead a few times and wrap in plastic wrap then into the refrigerator for at least an hour before rolling out the crust for a more delicate pastry. Prick pastry with fork for either method.
7. Put aluminum foil over pastry and fill the bottom of the pastry shell with small beans and bake for 20 minutes.
8. Remove beans and foil and continue baking for another 10 minutes

Filling:

1. Increase oven temperature to 375 degrees Fahrenheit
2. Put 8-oz room temperature blue cheese in mixing bowl
3. Add 2 Tbls heavy cream
4. Add 3 anchovy fillets and blend with a fork until smooth
5. Spread onto cooled pastry
6. Cut 4 roma tomatoes into very thin slices and spread over cheese —overlapping a little is a key.
7. Sprinkle with olive oil and either 1 tsp dried or 1 Tbls fresh thyme
8. Bake at 375 degrees for approximately 30 minutes until tomatoes collapse

Serving: Let the tart cool to room temperature, remove from tart pan, cut into slices and place on serving plates.

*If you used salted butter, do not add salt

Coq Au Vin

1. Chop – (medium chop, between mince and coarse)
   2 cups yellow onions (approximately 2 large onions)
   1 cup of carrots (approximately 2 large carrots peeled).
   Open – 1 small can of tomato paste
   1 bottle of red wine (check Tim's suggested wine on page 47)
   1 16-oz can/carton of low sodium chicken stock
   Put in small bowl –
   4 bay leaves
   1 tsp dried (or 2 heaping tsp fresh) thyme
   1 tsp dried (or 2 heaping tsp fresh) oregano
   Put frozen pearl onions in colander to thaw and drain. Clean button mushrooms – cut stems off at base of mushroom and wipe with paper towel (do not rinse with water). If using larger mushrooms, cut to bite size pieces.

2. Chicken – rinse and pat dry, separate leg and thigh if joined, season with salt and pepper

3. Cut 4 slices of thick bacon into $\frac{1}{4}$ inch wide strips and cook over medium heat in large, heavy Dutch oven until nicely browned. Remove bacon and drain on paper towels.

4. Add chicken parts to pan (one layer and not touching each other) and brown on both sides (start with skin side down). Remove to plate and repeat until all are browned. If there is not enough bacon grease to brown, add olive oil.

5. Add the chopped onions and carrots and cook, stirring occasionally until tender (about 8 minutes). Add more oil if necessary.

6. Stir in, with onions and carrots, 4 heaping Tbls all-purpose flour, reduce to low heat and cook, stirring constantly, until flour just begins to turn light brown, about 5 minutes.

7. First stir in 2 heaping Tbls tomato paste, then add:
   1 bottle red wine
   2 cups chicken stock
   The spices from the small bowl
   Increase heat and bring to a boil, stirring occasionally

8. Add crumbled bacon pieces and chicken to pot along with any juices. Return to boil and reduce heat, cover and simmer for approximately 30 minutes.

9. During the time while the chicken cooks, heat 4 Tbls unsalted butter in large skillet, add onions (thawed and drained on paper towels) and cook, stirring over medium heat until lightly browned, about 5 minutes.

10. Add mushrooms and cook with onions for about 5 minutes, until tender and remove pan from heat.

11. When done, remove the cooked chicken from the Dutch oven and put in pan in oven at 175 degrees Fahrenheit to keep warm.

The entire Coq au Vin to this point could be made in advance, either earlier in the day and left at room temperature (sauce, chicken, onions, and mushrooms) or put in refrigerator overnight. If refrigerated, degrease the sauce by skimming the top. Take out of the refrigerator and bring to room temperature 3 hours before serving. The sauce will be finished just before serving. The onions and mushrooms are okay at room temperature, but the chicken should be covered with foil and put in a warm oven (175 degrees Fahrenheit) for about 30 minutes before serving.

12. Bring the sauce to a boil over high heat and reduce until semi-thick. Skim off any fat from the top of the sauce.

13. Add onions and mushrooms with all accumulated juices and heat

14. Taste and check for seasoning, add salt and pepper if necessary

Egg Noodles:

1. Prepare egg noodles as directed on package

Serving: Place a mound of noodles on each plate, add one leg and one thigh and put sauce with onions and mushrooms on top. Sprinkle with chopped parsley and serve.

Crème Brulee
(prepared one day in advance)

1. You will need 8 individual 6-oz ovenproof ramekins for serving

2. Preheat oven to 250 degrees Fahrenheit

3. Separate 8 eggs and put yolks into medium bowl. (save whites for other uses, they make a great no yolk omelet or meringues for pies for example)

4. Stir $\frac{1}{2}$ cup sugar into yolks

5. Heat 2 cups heavy cream to a simmer, do not boil

6. Gradually stir simmered cream into egg and sugar mixture

7. Strain mixture with fine mesh strainer into another bowl

8. Stir in $\frac{3}{4}$ tsp vanilla

9. Spoon or pour into the 8 ramekins

10. Place in large high sided baking pan with warm (not hot) water approximately $\frac{1}{3}$ the way up the ramekins

11. Place in oven and bake for 1 to $1\frac{1}{2}$ hours until custard is set but still slightly quivery in the center.

12. Remove the ramekins from the water bath and let cool to room temperature. Cover each with plastic wrap which touches the custard and refrigerate overnight.

Serving: Remove from refrigerator, remove plastic wrap and blot any liquid on top with paper towels. Caramelize by sprinkling top of custard with sugar and melt under a broiler or with a propane torch and serve.

Wine

Serve the same wine with dinner as used in the preparation of the Coq au Vin.

Tim suggests: French Burgundy

Alternatives: American Pinot Noir

(Tim's comment: this was a tough one because you can probably use just about any red wine for the coq au vin – Merlot, Cabernet Sauvignon etc.—in fact white wine is not unheard of either. Traditionally, French burgundy is used, but it tends to be expensive! One option is to cook with a less expensive pinot noir and drink the burgundy.)

NOTES

Cousin Jim Comes to Visit and Plants an Herb Garden

Jim Benjamin is my cousin Barb's husband and the self-proclaimed chili king of Cincinnati. Jim and Barb have been regular guests at Sunny Shores for many years. Jim usually comes a week or two ahead while Barb finishes teaching the school year. Every summer, Jim makes a large batch of his special chili for the crowd. He spends the morning chopping, dicing, braising, and mixing ingredients and then lets the chili simmer, sometimes for two days, before he declares it ready to eat. Delicious.

Besides being a good cook, Jim can fix anything and has a great green thumb. I always make a list over the winter of projects for Jim to do in the spring. Two years ago, he decided we needed an herb garden. We now have three separate gardens that produce enough herbs for the neighborhood. There's always basil, rosemary, thyme, flat leaf parsley, sage, and cilantro. Jim also puts in a couple of tomato plants. (He brags about his homegrown tomatoes in Ohio, but who can't grow tomatoes in Ohio?) It is one of the great pleasures of summer, having fresh herbs and tomatoes right outside the kitchen door. After Jim has spent the afternoon digging and planting the garden, I always fix one of his favorite meals. Menu VI is one of those meals.

I wanted to include Jim's recipe for Chili in the book but he doesn't use one.

Menu VI

Cousin Jim's Menu
(6 servings)

Tomato Basil Salad

Beef Stroganoff with Onions, Mushrooms, and Peas

Vanilla Ice Cream Goblet with Rum

This is probably the easiest menu in this series and that fits right into a casual "dinner on the porch." It can easily be expanded to serve 8, 10, or 12.

Shopping List

Appetizer

2 large home grown (or vine-ripened) tomatoes

1 large Vidalia onion

1 bunch fresh basil

Small wedge parmesan cheese

Balsamic vinegar and olive oil

Coarse salt (Kosher or sea salt)

Freshly ground black pepper

Main Course

2 lbs. sirloin steak about 1 inch thick

1 package frozen pearl onions

1 package fresh button mushrooms

1 package frozen baby peas

8-oz low sodium beef stock

$\frac{1}{2}$ cup sour cream

1 medium Vidalia onion

2 Tbls cognac

1 package egg noodles

1 tsp Dijon mustard

6 Tbls butter

Parsley for garnish (optional)

Dessert

$\frac{1}{2}$ gallon good vanilla ice cream

Dark rum

Ground instant coffee

Tomato Basil Salad

1. Cut tomatoes into $\frac{1}{8}$ inch slices

2. Cut onion into $\frac{1}{8}$ inch slices

3. Roll basil leaves together and cut crosswise into chiffonade

Serving:

Alternate 3 slices tomato and onion on plate

Sprinkle with basil chiffonade

Use a potato peeler to put thin shavings of parmesan cheese on top

Sprinkle with a few drops of balsamic vinegar and olive oil

Top with a little coarse salt and freshly ground black pepper

NOTES

Beef Stroganoff

1. Put steak into freezer about 20 minutes which will make it much easier to cut

2. Slice into $\frac{1}{4}$ inch wide strips about 2 inches long

3. Thaw the frozen pearl onions and drain on paper towels

4. Clean and prepare mushrooms (if using large mushrooms, cut into bite size pieces)

5. Dice Vidalia onion into small pieces

6. In a large pan on mid/high heat, melt 3 Tbls butter and sauté onions and mushrooms for approximately 5 minutes

7. Remove from pan and set aside

8. Add and melt 3 Tbls butter

9. Sauté the diced onion for 5 minutes and remove

10. Add the sliced beef in batches and sauté each batch for 3 minutes and remove. The beef should remain reddish in the center.

11. Add 2 Tbls cognac and stir

12. Add 1 Tbls all-purpose flour and stir for 2 minutes

13. Add 8-oz beef stock and stir

14. Cook until thickened

15. Add mushroom-onion mixture and beef and diced onion

16. Add 1 package frozen peas

17. Heat thoroughly, reduce heat and keep warm

18. Prepare egg noodles according to package

19. Add $\frac{1}{2}$ cup sour cream and 1 tsp Dijon mustard to meat sauce, stir

20. Check seasoning, salt and pepper to taste

Serving: Serve noodles and sauce in separate bowls family style with chopped parsley for garnish.

Ice Cream Goblets

Put 1 or 2 large scoops of vanilla ice cream into large goblets or coffee cups, top with 2 to 3 Tbls dark rum and sprinkle with powdered instant coffee. Serve

Wine

Tim suggests: Cahors (French)

Alternatives: Argentine or Chilean Malbec, American Zinfandel

(Comment: Cahors is not too easy to find, but Malbecs are. Beef Stroganoff definitely calls for a robust red wine. This is not going to go well with the salad, so you might hold off serving it until the main course. Tomatoes are very hard to match with wine!)

Debby Hosts Our First Cooking Class And Receives A Whisk

Debby Cenname and I both worked at the old Crystal Beach Resort when we were teenagers. She worked there a few years after I did but we always love comparing stories about our experiences. Seven days a week Debby did laundry, cleaned cabins, and staffed the front desk. I taught guests to water ski, cleaned up the grounds, and did some of the cooking. I think I made about $35 a week but at least I was outdoors most of the day. It also provided me with a connection to several wonderful people over the years, Debby being one of them, so I was delighted when she agreed to host our first cooking class in June of 2008.

When I went over to Debby's to plan our class, I was surprised to learn that the lovely kitchen in her beautiful Lake Michigan home was a total mystery to her. I quickly saw that I would need to bring just about all the pans and utensils required for the class. The one thing I didn't bring was a whisk, assuming everyone has one. You guessed it, Debby did not own a whisk. I improvised by using one of the beaters out of the mixer and everyone loved that. I couldn't have hoped for a better start to our first season of Dinner on the Porch Cooking Classes. Every class sold out for the rest of the summer.

Menu VII is the menu we did for that first class Debby hosted. (I gave Debby a whisk as a thank you gift.)

Menu VII

Cooking Class Menu
(6 servings)

**Spinach Salad with Crisp Bacon, Roasted Pecans,
Mandarin Orange Slices with Vinaigrette Dressing
and Parmesan Crisps**

**Poached Salmon with Dill Cream and
Dijon Mustard Caper Sauces**

Smashed Red Potatoes with Peas and Pearl Onions

Fresh Berries with Sour Cream and Golden Brown Sugar

Poaching is probably the finest and most elegant way to prepare salmon and poached salmon can be served warm, at room temperature or chilled. Therefore, it can be poached ahead in a court bouillon and served chilled or at room temperture–do not re-heat. The shopping list and preparation included here is for six people; however, this menu can easily be adjusted to serve two or just as easily for eight.

Shopping List

Appetizer

1 package baby spinach

1 can mandarin orange segments

1 pound bacon, preferably thick sliced

8 to 10 ozs pecan halves

Parmesan Cheese, 10 to 12 oz fresh (no green cans please)

Dressing

$\frac{1}{3}$ cup balsamic vinegar (cider or other vinegars will work)

1 heaping tsp Dijon mustard

$\frac{1}{4}$ tsp fresh Tarragon (dried will work)

1 cup olive oil

Main Course

6 6-oz salmon fillets (you can have your fish monger cut this for.you or buy a whole fillet and cut yourself—check for pin bones)

Court bouillon for poaching requires: onions, celery, carrots, leeks, white wine, bay leaf, thyme, and parsley

Sauces

1 16-oz carton sour cream (dual use - sauce and dessert)

1 Tbls fresh dill (plus extra sprigs for garnish if desired)

1 4-oz package cream cheese

2 Tbls mayonnaise

1 heaping Tbls capers

Heavy cream, 1 pint (also for the potatoes)

White pepper

Potatoes

12 medium or 18 small red potatoes

1 package frozen peas

1 package frozen pearl onions

2 Tbls butter

Heavy cream

Dessert

1 box golden brown sugar

2 pints fresh berries (raspberries, blueberries, strawberries, etc.—your preference)

Sour cream (balance of 16-oz carton used in sauces)

Spinach Salad

Parmesan Crisps:

1. Grate parmesan cheese with semi-fine grater

2. Preheat oven to 350 degrees Fahrenheit

3. Place heaping tablespoons of the grated parmesan cheese on a low sided non-stick baking pan. If you have a "Silpat", use it because *nothing* will stick to it.

4. Bake for about 15 to 20 minutes or until golden brown.

5. Remove from pan and cool on oven rack.

Salad:

1. Wash and dry spinach (if not already done so in package)

2. Use 350 degree preheated oven from crisps and roast pecans on same pan for 10 to 15 minutes. Stir once or twice and be careful not to burn. (do not use silpat)

3. Use same low sided or non-stick pan without silpat and arrange bacon (not touching) in one layer and bake, about 20 minutes, until crisp. Remove to paper towels and let cool.

Dressing:

1. Place $\frac{1}{3}$ cup balsamic (or your preferred vinegar) in a bowl with 1 heaping tsp of Dijon mustard, $\frac{1}{2}$ tsp salt, $\frac{1}{4}$ tsp black pepper and $\frac{1}{4}$ tsp dried (or fresh) tarragon. Mix well.

2. Slowly add 1 cup good olive oil while whisking (you could also put all of this into a closed jar and shake briskly)

Serving: Place handful of spinach on each plate, sprinkle with roasted pecans, crumbled bacon and mandarin orange segments. Shake or stir dressing and drizzle lightly over salad. Place 1 or 2 parmesan crisps on each plate and serve.

NOTES

Dill Cream Sauce

1. Mix 8-oz sour cream and 2 Tbls mayonnaise with 1 Tbls minced fresh dill, and a pinch of salt and white pepper.

2. Cover and refrigerate until ready for use.

Mustard Caper Sauce

1. Put 4-oz cream cheese (at room temp) into food processor; while running, add heavy cream until thick, pourable mixture occurs. Add 1 Tbls Dijon mustard, pinch of salt and white pepper and blend.

2. Put into bowl, add 1 heaping Tbls drained capers, stir, cover, and refrigerate until ready for use.

Salmon

1. Check salmon for pin bones. Cut into serving pieces and poach with skin side down. You can remove skin carefully and easily after poaching.

2. Court bouillon:

   Combine in large pot over medium heat:

   a. 4 cups cold water

   b. $\frac{1}{2}$ cup coarsely chopped onions

   c. $\frac{1}{4}$ cup coarsely chopped leeks, white part only

   d. $\frac{1}{2}$ cup coarsely chopped celery

   e. $\frac{1}{4}$ cup coarsely chopped carrots

   f. 1 bouquet garni (use 3 long green parts of the leeks, put one small bunch of parsley, 3 to 4 sprigs of fresh thyme, 1 bay leaf, and 2 or 3 celery leaves into the leek leaves. Tie the leaves together with cotton twine.)

Bring mixture to a boil, reduce heat and simmer for about 20 minutes. Add 2 cups of the same white wine you will be serving with dinner and simmer for another 10 minutes. Season with 1 tsp salt and $\frac{1}{4}$ tsp ground black pepper. Strain into clean container. This can be made 1 to 2 days in advance and stored in the refrigerator or used immediately.

3. Poaching salmon:

    a. Put salmon into fish poacher or high sided roasting pan or very large (wide) soup pot so that all fillets rest on bottom (not stacked) skin side down.

    b. Pour warm (room temperature if made ahead) court bouillon over fish and bring to boil over high heat. Immediately remove from heat and let stand for 10 minutes.

    c. Remove fish and drain.

    d. Let cool slightly and remove skin. It can be served now or left at room temperature for 2 to 3 hours or refrigerated for use the next day (either serve chilled or at room temperature, do not reheat at this point).

Smashed Potatoes

1. Place frozen peas and pearl onions in a colander to thaw, approximately one hour.

2. Place 18 small or 12 medium (cut in half), red potatoes (with skins on) into large pot, cover with cold water and 1 Tbls salt. Bring to boil, reduce heat and simmer for about 20 minutes or until potatoes are cooked soft (a fork or knife inserted goes in and comes out easily). Drain and put back in pan over medium heat for about 2 minutes to get rid of excess water.

3. Add peas and onions to warm potatoes

4. Add 2 Tbls butter and $\frac{1}{2}$ cup heavy cream to pot and mash with hand masher to semi-smooth but lumpy mixture. Season with salt and pepper to taste. Keep warm on low heat until ready to serve. This could also be done hours in advance and kept warm in a double boiler (add a little more butter if needed)

Serving: Put the sauces into serving dishes with spoons. Put 1 piece of salmon on each plate and 2 small scoops of the potato mixture, garnish with a sprig of fresh dill and serve.

Fresh Berries with Sour Cream and Golden Brown Sugar

I've used several kinds of berries when preparing this dish. Blueberries, strawberries, and red raspberries are three of my favorites. I've also used Michigan peaches when they're in season-delicious.

1. Prepare berries (your choice) and cut as necessary into bite size pieces. Place berries into individual serving bowls.

2. Put a large dollop of sour cream (balance of 16-oz container used in dill cream sauce) on top of berries.

3. Sprinkle 1 heaping Tbls of golden brown sugar over sour cream and berries and serve.

Wine

Tim suggests: Austrian Riesling or Gruner Veltliner

Alternatives: New Zealand or American Sauvignon Blanc, Entre-Deux-Mers (white Bordeaux)

If you prefer red: Valpolicella

Betsie And Bob Come to Dinner and
Bob Has Two Desserts

Betsie Hosick is another of my longtime, Crystal Lake friends. I've known Betsie since we were kids and fondly remember having hotdogs and s'mores on her beach every summer. Betsie's grandparents started coming to this area in the early 1900s, one of the first families on the lake. Her grandparents, Dr. Paul and Elizabeth Oliver, were very civic-minded and did much for the community including donating money for the local hospital, now the Paul Oliver Memorial Hospital. Elizabeth Oliver was an artist and started the Crystal Lake Art Center that is still growing and going strong today.

Betsie has carried on the family tradition by becoming a doctor herself and very generously supporting both the hospital and the art center. We appreciate all the things Betsie has done for the community but one of the other things we appreciate about her is that she introduced us to her companion, Bob Weber. Bob and Betsie often attend our dinners on the porch, always adding a spark and bit of fun. Bob always has a good quip or story to entertain the guests and is quick to remind people to bring more than their appetites to dinner. Betsie keeps a close watch on their diets so one of the only chances Bob gets to cheat is at our dinners. He says it's the only time he tastes butter, sugar or cream and has been known to take a second dessert when Betsie isn't looking. This is especially true when I'm serving the chocolate mousse included in Menu VIII.

Menu VIII

Two Dessert Menu
(4 servings)

Spinach Flan

Marinated Roast Chicken

Roasted Root Vegetables

Chocolate Mousse

This whole meal is very easy to prepare and is great for "dinner on the porch". You can double or triple the recipes easily and most of the work is done one day in advance. The chicken is marinated overnight and the dessert needs at least six hours to overnight to set up. The marinated roast chicken recipe is courtesy of Jeri Richardson, Houston, Texas.

Shopping List

Appetizer

9-oz fresh spinach (buy a bag of pre-washed baby spinach)

8-oz sour cream

1 dozen eggs (dual use)

Nutmeg (preferably freshly ground)

8 slices bacon

Coarse salt (kosher or sea salt)

Spinach leaves for garnish, if desired

Main Course

1 4 to 5-pound roasting chicken

1 bottle dry white wine such as pinot grigio (red wine can also be used, see wine suggestions)

$\frac{1}{2}$ cup orange juice (preferably fresh squeezed or "not from concentrate")

10 cloves of garlic

1 bunch each of fresh parsley, thyme, oregano

8 small red potatoes

4 carrots

4 small turnips

4 stalks celery

1 cup olive oil

Dessert

7-oz bittersweet chocolate

1 vanilla bean

Whipping cream

3 large eggs

2 Tbls unsalted butter

2 Tbls sugar

Spinach Flan

1. Cut 8 bacon slices into approximately $\frac{1}{4}$ inch pieces and brown in large skillet

2. Remove bacon and drain on paper towel, reserving grease in pan

3. Add spinach in batches to hot bacon grease and cook only until spinach wilts. (add olive oil if there is not enough grease)

4. Put all spinach in a colander to drain off any excess grease

5. Put in large bowl and beat well:
   a. 2 large eggs
   b. $\frac{3}{4}$ cup sour cream
   c. $\frac{1}{4}$ tsp coarse salt (kosher or sea salt)
   d. $\frac{1}{16}$ tsp freshly grated nutmeg (ground is ok but fresh is better)

The recipe can be done a few hours in advance to this point

6. Preheat oven to 350 degrees Fahrenheit

7. Chop the spinach coarsely if the leaves are too big and stir into the egg mixture

8. Add the bacon bits and stir

9. Butter the bottom of a 2-quart shallow baking dish

10. Put spinach mixture into dish and bake for approximately 25 to 30 minutes until mixture is just set.

Serving: Serve hot or at room temperature. Spoon onto small plates and garnish with a few fresh spinach leaves.

Chicken Marinade

1. Take giblets out of chicken and freeze for future use or cook for your cat or dog.

2. Rinse chicken under cold water and put in a large (1 gallon) sealable plastic bag

3. Put the following on the chicken in the bag:
   a. 1 cup olive oil
   b. 1 cup white wine
   c. $\frac{1}{2}$ cup orange juice
   d. 10 smashed garlic cloves (ok to leave skin on cloves)
   e. 1 bunch parsley – bruised (bruised means "hit" (not chop) with the back of a knife or the bottom of a pan. This helps to release the flavor of the herbs).
   f. 1 bunch thyme – bruised
   g. 1 bunch oregano – bruised
   h. 1 tsp salt
   i. 1 tsp pepper

4. Seal bag and lightly massage to mix all ingredients

5. Refrigerate overnight in a pan to catch any possible leeks or drips

Roasting:

6. Take chicken from refrigerator 1 hour before roasting and put marinated herbs into cavity.

7. Prepare root vegetables:
   a. Wash potatoes (cut in half if too large)
   b. Peel carrots and cut to about same size as potatoes
   c. Peel and cut turnips the same
   d. Peel and cut celery the same
   e. Put all root vegetables in large bowl and lightly coat with olive oil, salt and pepper

8. Put chicken, breast side up, in large shallow sided roasting pan and scatter all root vegetables around pan.

9. Put in a pre-heated, 350 degree Fahrenheit oven and roast for 1 to $1\frac{1}{2}$ hours depending on size of chicken (you can baste periodically with melted butter for richer, more golden chicken)

10. Let rest for 15 minutes before serving. While the chicken is resting, you could skim the fat from the roasting pan, put the pan on the stove and add a little more wine to deglaze, then add a little butter or cream and use as a light au jus.

Serving: You have 2 choices:

1. Put whole chicken and vegetables on a large serving platter and carve at the table

2. Same as above, but just show everyone what it looks like and then carve in the kitchen and serve plated.

For this recipe for four, I would serve each leg and thigh as one serving and each breast half and wing as one serving.

NOTES

Chocolate Mousse
(reminder, this recipe only serves 4)

This needs to be done in the morning or the day before so it can set-up properly. You can use four 8-oz soufflé cups or four regular coffee cups or four small bowls.

1. Cut 2 Tbls unsalted butter into small pieces and bring to room temperature

2. Cut vanilla bean lengthwise and scrape out the seeds with sharp knife. You use the seeds only, discard the bean pod. (you could use $\frac{1}{2}$ tsp pure vanilla extract in place of bean)

3. Separate 3 large eggs.

4. Put 7-oz bittersweet chocolate and the 2 Tbls butter in a medium size bowl and melt in the microwave on high – do this in 30 second intervals and stir in between (just melt, do not cook)

5. Add the vanilla seeds and 3 egg yolks and stir

6. In a separate bowl, beat egg whites and a pinch of salt with mixer until semi-stiff. Gradually add 2 Tbls sugar and beat until firm.

7. Using a spatula, gradually fold the stiff egg whites into the chocolate mixture. Make sure no white specks can be seen.

8. Put the mousse into the serving dishes and refrigerate for at least 6 hours, but overnight is better. Cover mousse in dishes with plastic wrap touching the mousse. (this keeps a film from forming on top of the mousse)

Serving: Take mousse out of the refrigerator when starting the meal and serve with a dollop of whipped cream if desired (why not go all the way!)

Wine

Tim suggests: Rioja (Spanish)

Alternatives: Minervois (Southern France),
Australian Shiraz

If you prefer white: Pinot Grigio (recommended
for the marinade), American Viognier

NOTES

Marjorie's Secret Dinner

Despite her lack of cooking skills (see Menu III), Marjorie Elliott has become a close friend. She's also been the main force behind this cookbook and the cooking classes. When I heard she was having three of her girlfriends visit Crystal Lake for the week, I suggested that I prepare an arrival dinner and leave it ready for service at her home while she picked up her friends at the airport. I also said she should let her friends assume she did the preparation. I think we may have gotten away with our secret if I had not made the presentation display as grand and elegant as I did. I over did it and, well, her friends know her too well.

One of the items I prepared was the following gravlax recipe in Menu IX.

Menu IX

Secret Dinner Menu
(8 servings)

Gravlax with Cocktail Rye and Mustard Cream

**Crown Roast of Pork with Chutney
and Sage Stuffing with Dried Cherries**

Steamed Asparagus

Floating Islands

It's hard to beat prime rib and Yorkshire pudding but, this will do it. The presentation is exceptional and the flavor is, well, great. Save this for a dinner party where you want to impress everyone and it is really not very hard to create. A full crown roast easily serves 8 to 10 so you may have some very tasty left over pork. The dessert looks like you've spent hours at the last minute and have a cook in the kitchen, but is actually prepared the day in advance. The gravlax is also prepared in advance.

Shopping List

Appetizer

2 salmon fillets about 2 lbs each with skin left on

2 bunches fresh dill

Brandy, 3 to 4 Tbls

Mayonnaise (10 oz)

$2\frac{1}{2}$ cups coarse salt (Kosher or sea salt)

$1\frac{1}{2}$ cups sugar

1 Tbls Dijon mustard

Cocktail-style Rye bread slices

Decorative lettuce leaves (optional)

Main Course

1 pork crown roast, approximately 8 lbs (your butcher will prepare this for you if you give him a little advanced notice)

Fresh or dried oregano

2 lbs fresh asparagus

1 large loaf sliced white bread (you can substitute whole wheat)

1 bunch celery

1 large sweet onion

2 cans low sodium chicken broth

Rubbed dry sage

1 package dried cherries

1 jar mango chutney

Olive oil for rubbing meat

2 Tbls butter

Dessert

For meringue:

12 egg whites

$\frac{1}{2}$ tsp cream of tartar

$1\frac{1}{2}$ cups sugar

2 tsp pure vanilla extract

For custard:

6 egg yolks

$\frac{2}{3}$ cup sugar

$1\frac{1}{4}$ cups milk

$1\frac{1}{2}$ Tbls pure vanilla extract

2 Tbls unsalted butter

3 to 4 Tbls dark rum (optional)

Gravlax
(<u>must</u> be made 2 to 3 days in advance of dinner)

Make sure salmon fillets are boneless; especially all pin bones are removed. Rub your hand all over meat side to check for pin bones. Cut off any excess fat along belly edge of fillet.

Mix together:

    2 $\frac{1}{2}$ cups coarse salt (Kosher or Sea Salt)

    1 $\frac{1}{2}$ cups sugar

    1 tablespoon ground black pepper

Coarsely chop fresh dill and set aside – save one Tbls of finely chopped dill for sauce

Use a casserole pan large enough to hold one fillet without folding. Line casserole with enough plastic wrap to fold over the top and seal the ends.

1. Spread about $\frac{1}{4}$ of the salt/sugar mixture on the plastic wrap

2. Place one fillet, skin side down, on mixture

3. Spread $\frac{1}{4}$ of the mixture on meat side of fillet

4. Put chopped dill on top of salt

5. Sprinkle with about 3 to 4 Tbls of brandy

6. Spread another $\frac{1}{4}$ mixture on top of dill

7. Place second fillet, meat side down, on top of mixture

8. Spread balance of mixture over skin side of fillet

9. Fold plastic wrap in on all 4 sides

10. Put a smaller casserole on top of wrapped salmon and place a 3 to 4lb weight on top.
    Or, you can use 2 bricks wrapped in plastic and foil right on top of fish without the extra casserole.

11. Put in refrigerator and let sit for 2 to 3 days. Turn the fish package over at least once a day. Gravlax is done when meat is opaque, usually 3 days, but depending on thickness, it could be ready in 2 days.

12. Quickly rinse mixture off salmon with cold water and wrap in plastic. Keep chilled.

Mustard Cream:
Mix 1 cup mayonnaise with 1 Tbls Dijon mustard and 1 Tbls finely chopped dill

Serving: Slice gravlax as thinly as possible, cutting on the bias, without cutting through the skin. Put both sliced fillets on a large platter covered with decorative lettuce leaves and serve with the mustard sauce and cocktail ryes.

Crown Roast Pork and Stuffing

The night before – cut open the bread package and spread so that bread dries slightly. Do not totally dry bread.

Take crown roast from refrigerator 2 hours before roasting so it comes to room temperature. (It will take approximately 2 $\frac{1}{2}$ hours to cook) Rub entire roast with olive oil and lightly coat with salt, pepper, and oregano. Put directly into low sided roasting pan with no rack.

While roast is resting before roasting, take partially dried bread and break into bite size pieces (including crusts) and put into large bowl.

1. Cut onion into medium dice

2. Cut 2 to 3 stalks celery into medium dice

3. Sauté onion and celery in 2 Tbls butter with 1 tsp salt and $\frac{1}{2}$ tsp pepper for 15 minutes

4. Add 1 heaping Tbls sage

5. Add 1 package dried cherries

6. Pour mixture over bread and mix

7. Add chicken broth slowly until mixture is damp (but not soggy, this is to taste)

8. Cover with clean towel and set aside

Roast – Preheat oven to 375 degrees Fahrenheit

1. Roast for approx 20 minutes per pound

2. After first hour, fill cavity with bread dressing and continue roasting*

3. Remove from oven when internal temperature reaches 160 degrees Fahrenheit

4. Cover with foil and let rest for 15 minutes

*If cavity will not hold stuffing, place stuffing in a casserole dish and bake for 30 minutes at 400 degrees Fahrenheit.

Asparagus

Cooking time is approximately 5 minutes for firm spears. You can prepare asparagus in advance for last minute steaming.

1. Break each spear where it naturally breaks when snapped.*

2. Rinse in cold water and wrap in dampened paper towels until ready to cook

3. In a large pan or skillet where all spears can lie flat on the bottom, bring about $\frac{1}{2}$ inch of chicken broth to a boil.

4. Add 1 tsp salt

5. Add asparagus, cover and cook for approximately 5 minutes or until desired doneness

Serving: The crown roast pork can be easily carved and served at the table for a terrific presentation. The rack slices easily into individual chops. Add a spoonful of the dressing and a few asparagus spears. Serve with mango chutney on the side.

*If using fresh Michigan asparagus, you do not need to break off the ends.

NOTES

Floating Islands
(May be completely made 1 day in advance)

Meringue:

1. Preheat oven to 250 degrees Fahrenheit
2. Heavily butter and dust with sugar a straight sided soufflé dish or casserole
3. Separate 12 eggs – put the whites into an electric mixer bowl and save the yolks for the custard
4. Put $\frac{1}{2}$ tsp cream of tartar and $\frac{1}{16}$ tsp salt in small bowl
5. Put $1\frac{1}{2}$ cups sugar in small bowl
6. Put 2 tsp pure vanilla extract in small bowl
7. Start beating the egg whites at moderate speed until foamy
8. Add cream of tartar and salt, increase speed
9. Beat to soft peaks
10. Slowly add sugar and beat until stiff peaks
11. Add vanilla and beat until mixed
12. Scoop into baking dish
13. Bake for 35 to 40 minutes until a skewer inserted to bottom comes out clean. Over-bake rather than under-bake
14. Cool to room temperature, cover and refrigerate

Custard:

1. Put 6 saved egg yolks into mixing bowl (save the other 6 for richer scrambled eggs or double this recipe and freeze half for later use)
2. Beat in $\frac{2}{3}$ cup sugar until mixture is pale
3. Heat $1\frac{1}{2}$ cups milk to boiling point
4. Slowly add hot milk to egg mixture
5. Transfer to non-stick pan and heat, stirring until mixture thickens

6. Remove from heat, add 1 $\frac{1}{2}$ Tbls pure vanilla extract and 2 Tbls unsalted butter (plus 3 to 4 Tbls dark rum if desired) and beat vigorously with whisk to cool. (this can be served hot, warm or cold)

7. Cover and refrigerate for this recipe

Serving: Unmold meringue by running knife around edge of dish and giving a slap to the bottom of the pan onto a large platter. Pour custard around and serve by either slicing or spooning onto individual plates with custard.

Wine

Tim suggests: Bairrada (Portuguese). For the gravlax, shots of ice-cold aquavit or vodka!

Alternatives: Ribera del Duero (Spanish), Dao (Portuguese), Nemea (Greek), French Bordeaux

If you prefer white: French Burgundy, non-oaky American Chardonnay

CRYSTAL VIEW CAFE

Jim Cooks His Own Thank You Dinner

At the end of last summer Pete and Amy Taylor wanted to give a thank you dinner for all the Crystal View guest chefs. Guess who got to cook for the dinner for twelve in his little kitchen. Amy went to Sam's Club and purchased a 16 pound prime rib roast which wouldn't fit in my oven in one full piece. I had to cut it off the bone to get it in the oven. The following menu was prepared with the exception of the Yorkshire Pudding—it was substituted by a large, wild puffball mushroom which Kim Fairchild found in the woods adjacent to his summer cottage.

Note: I like to prepare puffball mushrooms by simply slicing them and sautéing in butter.

Menu X

Thank You Dinner
(6 to 8 servings)

Vidalia Onion Tart

Roast Prime Rib of Beef—Au Jus and Horseradish Cream

Yorkshire Pudding

Roasted Brussels Sprouts

Summer Berry Pudding

The "king of beef" is the standing prime rib slow roasted to medium rare for the juiciest, most succulent piece of meat you have ever tasted. You can order a prime rib roast of almost any size but we don't recommend less than about 4 pounds. This recipe is a guide for 6 to 8 servings. Plan for 6 and have the rest left for sandwiches the next day and serve the bones for midnight snacks. They're too good for the dog. Yorkshire pudding replaces potatoes and is a traditional accompaniment. You can replace the Brussels sprouts with green beans if desired.

Shopping List

Appetizer

3 medium size Vidalia onions

2 large Eggs

$\frac{1}{2}$ cup heavy cream

Nutmeg

Ready made pastry (you can cheat and buy ready made pastry, but it's not hard to make yourself)

3 Tbls butter

Main Course

One standing rib beef roast about 5 to 6 pounds

Lawry's Seasoned Salt

Prepared horseradish

8-oz sour cream

8-oz low sodium beef broth or beef consommé

Paprika

2 large eggs

1 cup Milk

32 to 40 medium sized Brussels sprouts (4 to 5 per person)

Olive oil

Black pepper

1 cup all-purpose flour

Dessert

1 pint fresh strawberries, or 12-oz package frozen strawberries

1 pint fresh blueberries or 12-oz frozen

1 pint raspberries or 12-oz frozen (you can substitute any berries of your choice)

2 lemons

2 pound cakes

1 pint heavy whipping cream

Vidalia Onion Tart

1. Preheat oven to 400 degrees Fahrenheit

2. Either use a pre-made single crust pastry and line a tart pan or make from scratch as shown in Menu V appetizer (put pastry lined tart pan in refrigerator until ready to bake)

3. Thinly slice 3 medium size Vidalia onions

4. Melt 3 Tbls butter in medium skillet over medium heat and cook (not fry) onions until soft and lightly browned. Season with $\frac{1}{2}$ tsp salt and $\frac{1}{4}$ tsp pepper while cooking, about 15 to 20 minutes. Let cool.

5. Custard – In a medium mixing bowl beat 2 large eggs with whisk until smooth.

   Add $\frac{1}{2}$ cup heavy cream

   Add $\frac{1}{4}$ tsp freshly grated or ground nutmeg

   Add $\frac{1}{4}$ tsp salt and $\frac{1}{8}$ tsp pepper, or to taste

   Mix well

6. Spread cooled onions in tart shell

7. Pour custard over onions

8. Bake until golden, about 20 to 30 minutes

9. Let the tart cool for at least 15 minutes, or to room temperature, and cut into wedges and serve.

This can easily be prepared up to one day in advance and served at room temperature. (Refrigerate overnight if made the day before, or if you make it more than four hours in advance).

NOTES

Prime Rib Roast

NOTES

1. Take prime rib from refrigerator at least 6 hours, or up to 12 hours, in advance of roasting and rub all over lightly with olive oil. Season heavily with Lawry's Seasoned Salt and black pepper. Place on rack in roasting pan, rib side down. Sprinkle meat side with all-purpose flour to coat and sprinkle lightly with paprika.

2. Cover the roast lightly with foil and let rest at room temperature until ready to roast.

3. Roasting

   a. Preheat oven to 450 degrees Fahrenheit

   b. Roast uncovered for 10 minutes

   c. Reduce oven to 250 degrees Fahrenheit

   d. Roast as follows:

      i. Rare- approximately 20 minutes per pound, internal temperature 120 degrees to 130 degrees

      ii. Medium rare- approximately 25 minutes per pound, internal temperature 130 degrees to 140 degrees

      iii. Medium- approximately 30 minutes per pound, internal temperature 145 degrees to 160 degrees

   e. Remove the roast from oven, put it on a platter and cover loosely with foil for 15 to 30 minutes before serving.

Au Jus

1. Remove roasting rack from pan.

2. Remove excess grease from the roasting pan (it's ok to leave a small amount in the pan) and save it for the Yorkshire pudding

3. Put roasting pan on stove at medium heat

4. Add $\frac{1}{2}$ to $\frac{3}{4}$ cup beef stock (broth) or preferably beef consummé.

5. Bring to a boil and scrape bottom of pan to dissolve pan drippings. Salt and pepper to taste.

6. Strain into pan and keep warm until served.

Horseradish Cream

1. Mix 8-oz sour cream with 2 to 4 Tbls horseradish and salt and pepper to taste

Roasted Brussels Sprouts

1. Cut a small piece off the root end and remove any damaged or loose leaves.

2. Put sprouts in large bowl containing 1 Tbls salt dissolved in 4 cups water and let stand at room temperature for at least 2 hours. They can sit all day.

Roasting – the sprouts will roast with the Yorkshire pudding while the prime rib rests after taking it from the oven.

3. Preheat oven to 400 degrees Fahrenheit

4. Drain water from bowl

5. Drizzle sprouts with $\frac{1}{4}$ cup olive oil and toss

6. Season lightly with Lawry's seasoned salt and black pepper and toss

7. Put into roasting pan (you can use the pan from the meat without cleaning) and put in oven. Bake for 30 minutes. They should be lightly browned and soft.

Yorkshire Pudding
(cooks at same temperature and time as sprouts*)

1. In medium bowl, whisk 2 eggs until frothy.

2. Add 1 cup milk and $\frac{1}{2}$ tsp salt and whisk

3. Gradually beat in 1 cup all-purpose flour until smooth. Batter is very thin, don't worry.

4. Use a non-stick muffin pan with at least 8 cups. Put a small amount, approximately 1 tsp, of the grease drippings from the roast in each cup and tilt to coat sides. (If you don't have enough roast drippings, add melted butter)

5. Put muffin pan in 400 degree oven for 5 minutes before filling

6. Pour approximately 3 Tbls of batter in each greased, hot cup and bake for 30 minutes, until light brown.

Serving: Carving the roast – if you want a dramatic service, put the roast, sprouts, and pudding on one large platter and carve and serve at the table. Of course, you need someone willing to take on the challenge, but it is spectacular. Otherwise, the easiest way to carve is to first cut the meat off the rib bones as close as possible to the bone (save for later or give to people you know will really enjoy the bone, which they will probably eat with their hands). Then carve the meat into the desired thickness, usually about $\frac{1}{2}$ inch thick slices. The center cuts will be less done then the ends, so medium rare interior will have medium end cuts.

Put one slice of beef on each plate along with some Brussels sprouts and one Yorkshire pudding just out of the oven. Serve immediately along with the au jus and horseradish cream.

*But put in oven 15 minutes later than the sprouts so they are done 15 minutes after the sprouts. This gives you time to carve and plate beef and sprouts before the pudding is done. The pudding needs to be served *immediately* after baking—do not let stand before serving.

Summer Berry Pudding

This needs to be made one day in advance and kept in the refrigerator until just before serving.

1. Use a $1\frac{1}{2}$ quart soufflé dish or broad, tall bowl

2. Line dish with plastic wrap, leaving enough on the sides to cover dish when finished

3. Remove the crusts and cut pound cake into $\frac{3}{8}$ inch slices

4. Cover the bottom of the dish with slices cut to fit.

5. Line the sides to the top of the dish, slightly overlapping the pieces.

6. Trim enough slices to make 2 layers inside and one to cover the top, reserve

7. In a large saucepan combine, over medium heat:
    a. 1 pint sliced strawberries
    b. 1 pint blackberries
    c. 1 pint raspberries
    d. 1 cup sugar
    e. 3 Tbls fresh squeezed lemon juice

8. Stir mixture until berries begin to release their juices. Do not bring to boil. Stir frequently. Take from heat and let cool to room temperature.

9. Spoon $\frac{1}{3}$ of mixture into pound cake lined dish

10. Put 1 reserved layer of pound cake on top of mixture and spread an additional $\frac{1}{3}$ mixture over pound cake layer

11. Repeat with another layer of pound cake and berry mixture

12. Put last layer of pound cake on top and cover with the plastic wrap which overlaps the dish.

13. Put a bowl or pan that is just slightly smaller than the soufflé dish or bowl on top and add approximately a 2 pound weight in bowl or pan

14. Put the entire contraption in a pan to catch any overflow juices and refrigerate for 12 to 24 hours.

Serving: Add 1 Tbls sugar and $\frac{1}{2}$ tsp vanilla extract to one pint heavy whipping cream and whip until firm and fluffy. Remove pudding from refrigerator. Take weight and pan from top of dish and open plastic wrap. Invert the pudding onto a platter and remove plastic wrap. Cut the pudding with a sharp knife or large shallow spoon and serve with a dollop of whipped cream and a sprig of mint if desired.

Wine

Tim suggests: Strongly recommends red Bordeaux (2005 was a good year)

Alternatives: American or Australian Cabernet Sauvignon

Crab Night Always Draws a Crowd

The small porch, 10' by 24', is the location of most of the activity in this sweet little cottage—dining, working, reading, cocktailing, talking. Dinner for eight seems crowded but the seams practically burst at Crab Night for eighteen. (I still can't figure out where we all sat.)

We used every available space for all the bottoms to sit including three or four on the daybed. Kate, Kim Fairchild's daughter, had brought us over twenty pounds of frozen crab several weeks before from Chicago. It took two freezers—ours and the Fairchild's—to store it. The night of the party we had newspapers on every horizontal surface. Smoking outside, please. But be careful not to let Bella and Luna, the two four-footed children out. Appetizers were bone marrow in the bone. We hadn't had any for years since being in France or Maxim's in Chicago. It was bought as pet treats in Beulah as it was way too expensive sold as human food.

But where did we seat 18? In several photos, I remember 18 fat crab legs being raised in salute to the chefs. Amy and Pete Taylor used a little birch footstool for their table. Everyone left sated and we had nary a leg for leftovers. The trash man must have wondered—all the bottles, newspapers, bones and shells.

Crab Night has become an annual event and usually includes one of the appetizers in the following section.

Suggested Substitutions for Appetizers

French Onion Soup, 90

Braised Leeks with Herb Vinaigrette, 91

Braised Celery, 92

Portabella Mushrooms Stuffed with Sausage, 94

The following pages contain additional recipes for appetizers. These are meant to be substitutions for the appetizers that are included in Menus I through X. For example, if you have someone that can't eat shellfish, you could substitute the French onion soup appetizer described in this section for the avocado stuffed with crabmeat included in Menu I. All will work beautifully. Enjoy.

French Onion Soup
(serves 6)

Shopping List

2 large red onions

2 large sweet onions

10-oz low sodium chicken broth

10-oz low sodium beef broth

10-oz unfiltered apple cider

1 bottle dry white wine

2-oz cognac

1 loaf French bread or baguette

6-oz Gruyere cheese

1 bay leaf

2 sprigs fresh thyme

Preparation

1. Slice the 4 onions thinly
2. Melt 2 Tbls butter and 1 Tbls olive oil in large saucepan
3. Add onions and cook over medium heat to caramelize, about 40 minutes, stirring frequently
4. Sprinkle 1 heaping Tbls flour over onions and stir
5. Add:
   a. Bay Leaf
   b. Thyme
   c. Chicken broth
   d. Beef broth
   e. Apple cider
   f. 10-oz dry white wine
   g. Season with 1 tsp salt and $\frac{1}{2}$ tsp pepper
6. Bring to a boil – reduce heat and simmer for 1 hour
7. Just before serving add 2-oz cognac and stir, remove bay leaf and any sprigs left from the thyme

Serving

1. Slice French bread or baguette into $\frac{1}{4}$ to $\frac{1}{2}$ inch slices
2. Lightly toast or brown in the oven under the broiler
3. Grate cheese
4. Ladle soup into individual oven proof bowls
5. Top with a slice of toast
6. Sprinkle with cheese
7. Cook under the broiler until cheese is browned and bubbly
8. Serve immediately with bread

Braised Leeks with Herb Vinaigrette
(serves 4)

Shopping List

4 large or 8 baby leeks

1 can low sodium chicken broth

Wine vinegar

Dijon mustard

Olive oil

1 bunch flat leaf parsley

1 bunch cilantro

1 bunch chives

2 shallots

Preparation - Vinaigrette

1. Put into blender and blend:
   a. $\frac{1}{4}$ cup wine vinegar
   b. 1 tsp Dijon mustard
   c. 1 tsp coarse salt
2. Add about $\frac{1}{3}$ cup olive oil and blend
3. Add remaining $\frac{2}{3}$ cup olive oil and blend until emulsified
4. Coarse chop and add:
   a. Handful of flat parsley (no long stems)
   b. Handful of cilantro (no long stems)
   c. $\frac{1}{2}$ tsp fresh ground black pepper
5. Blend and refrigerate until ready for use

Preparation - Leeks

1. Cut off bottom and top of green ends, leaving about 2 inches above the white section
2. If using large leeks, cut in half lengthwise (leave baby leeks whole)
3. Rinse under cold water checking for any dirt. Preserve halved leeks shape by tying each end with a piece of cotton string
4. Melt 2 Tbls butter and 1 Tbls olive oil in large skillet over medium/high heat and sauté leeks until lightly browned, about 3 minutes per side.
5. Add the can of chicken broth, bring to a boil, reduce heat to simmer, cover and cook for about 10 minutes until tender.
6. Remove from pan to paper towels to drain
7. Put leeks flat in large casserole dish
8. Blend vinaigrette once again and pour over leeks
9. Refrigerate for at least 1 hour or overnight

Serving: Put 2 baby leeks or two of the $\frac{1}{2}$ leeks on individual plates. Spoon vinaigrette over leeks. Garnish with the sliced shallots and chopped chives and serve.

Braised Celery
(Serves 6)

NOTES

Shopping List

2 whole celery bunches

2 slices bacon

1 large yellow onion

1 large carrot

2 cloves garlic

1 8-oz can peeled and diced tomatoes

1 bottle dry white wine

1 can flat anchovies (optional, but preferred)

1 bunch flat leaf parsley

1 bay leaf

Preparation

1. Cut off leafy ends of celery
2. Separate stalks and cut off heavy bottom end
3. Peel heavy ribs of celery with potato peeler. These peelings look like strings and are very tough.
4. Add enough water to cover celery to a large skillet with lid and bring water to a boil
5. Add 1 Tbls salt and put the celery ribs flat on bottom of pan - do not stack.
6. Cover and simmer gently for 10 minutes
7. Remove celery from pan and drain on paper towels, dump water.
8. Cut 3 slices bacon into thin strips
9. Peel and cut onion into quarters and slice thinly
10. Peel and cut carrot in half lengthwise and then slice thinly
11. Mince 2 garlic cloves with 1 tsp coarse salt
12. Heat 2 Tbls oil in the same large skillet
13. Add the following and sauté for 5 minutes:
    a. Bacon
    b. Onion
    c. Carrot

NOTES

14. Add the garlic and drained celery – sauté until celery is lightly browned
15. Add and bring to a boil:
    a. Tomatoes with juice
    b. 1 cup white wine
    c. 1 bay leaf
16. Reduce heat, cover and simmer for 30 minutes, turning celery over after 15 minutes
17. Remove celery to casserole and keep warm
18. Raise heat on pan and reduce sauce for about 10 minutes

Serving: Place 2 stalks of celery on each individual plate, pour some sauce over and sprinkle with chopped anchovies and chopped parsley. Serve (This can be served as a family style vegetable by serving it in a casserole dish with sauce and garni)

Portabella Mushrooms Stuffed with Sausage
(Serves 6)

Shopping List

6 medium or 18 small portabella mushrooms

½ lb Italian sausage – either mild or hot, your choice

1 small jar roasted red peppers or pimentos

Dry white wine

Dry bread crumbs

1 bunch cilantro

Parmesan cheese – wedge to grate fresh (not canned)

Decorative lettuce

Preparation – Mushrooms

1. Remove stems from mushrooms and save
2. Remove dark veins from mushrooms and discard
3. Wipe mushrooms with paper towel (do not rinse or use any water)
4. Coat mushrooms with 2 to 3 Tbls melted butter
5. Put mushrooms, cavity side down, on roasting pan and place under the broiler for 3 minutes
6. Remove and turn over ready for filling

Preparation – Filling

1. The following can all be chopped together in a food processor or done by hand
   a. Mince 1 large clove of garlic (If using hot sausage, no garlic is required)
   b. Drain and chop 3 Tbls roasted peppers or pimentos
   c. Chop 2 heaping Tbls cilantro
   d. Chop the saved mushroom stems
2. Heat 1 Tbls olive oil in medium size skillet
3. Add sausage and chopped mushroom mixture to skillet and sauté until sausage is lightly cooked (just until red color is gone)

4. Add and stir:
5. Chopped peppers
6. Chopped cilantro
7. ½ cup bread crumbs
8. Add 2 to 5 Tbls wine and stir (mixture should be damp but not sloshy)
9. Remove from heat

This can all be done in advance (even 1 day) to this point. Refrigerate if holding overnight.

Serving

1. Preheat oven to 375 degrees Fahrenheit
2. Fill mushroom cavities heaping with stuffing
3. Top with fresh grated parmesan cheese
4. Bake for about 15 minutes

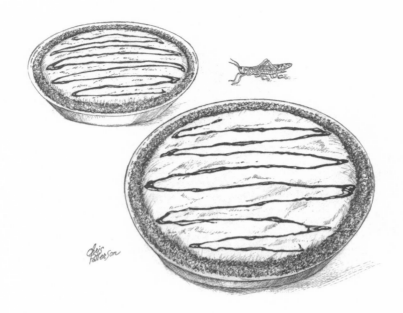

Lars Bakes Grasshopper Pie And Receives Four Marriage Proposals

Lars, as he often is, was called upon to provide dessert for one of our dinners on the porch. He decided this was a good chance to test out his newly developed Grasshopper Pie recipe. He didn't know how many people we would be serving so he made two pies. As luck would have it, one pie would do. Lars knew that Marjorie had four of her girlfriends as guests for the weekend, so guess where the other pie went? When Lars saw Marjorie several days later, she said the girls loved it. . . and all four of them asked for Lars' hand in marriage. How's that for dessert!

The recipe for this marriage-inspiring dessert is included here.

Suggested Substitutions for Desserts

The following pages contain additional recipes for desserts and are all provided by Larry "Lars" Hilton. These are meant to be substitutions for the desserts that are included in Menus I through X. Feel free to mix it up. All will work beautifully. Enjoy.

And remember, you can be very creative with food recipes, but baking is a science, not much wiggle room between perfection and . . . ugh!

Pound Cake

Pound cake the old way: one pound each of flour, sugar, eggs, and butter. We're not going to do that. Our pound cake, while still dense and moist, will be somewhat lighter.

Pound cake is a very versatile little morsel to have in any dessert arsenal. It's great on its own, wonderful when paired with various toppings, and is also often used as a platform for other desserts. Two of our dessert offerings call for pound cake as a base, which is why it appears here. Yes, you can buy it, but what fun is that? This recipe goes together fairly quickly, and scratch made cakes just taste better.

Shopping List

- 1 cup of butter (2 sticks) at room temperature
- 1 cup of granulated sugar
- 3 Tbls of light brown sugar, well packed
- $\frac{1}{2}$ tsp of salt (use table salt, not a more coarse grind)

- 1 tsp baking powder
- 1 Tbls pure vanilla extract
- $1\frac{3}{4}$ cups of all-purpose flour
- 4 large eggs at room temperature

Preparation

1. Combine 1 cup of butter, 1 cup of granulated sugar, 3 Tbls of well packed light brown sugar, $\frac{1}{2}$ tsp of salt, 1 tsp baking powder, and 1 Tbls pure vanilla extract in a large mixing bowl and beat until smooth and fluffy.

2. Add 1 $\frac{3}{4}$ cups of all-purpose flour a bit at a time, until well mixed. It helps to scrape down the edges and bottom of the mixing bowl several times while doing this. At this stage, you will have a very dense, pasty mixture.

3. Add 4 large eggs, one egg at a time until well incorporated, scraping down the edges and bottom of the bowl after adding each egg. The batter should now look to be fairly fluffy. The batter is dense.

4. Prepare your 9x5 inch loaf pan by lightly greasing the interior (no need to flour it). Pour the batter into the prepared pan and bake at 350 degrees Fahrenheit for about 45 to 50 minutes, until a tooth pick inserted into the middle of the cake comes out clean.

5. Take the cake out of the oven and place it on a cooling rack for at least 10 minutes.

6. Take a table knife and gently go around the edges of the cake pan, invert the pan and ease the cake out.

Serving: This flexible cake can be served on its own or with a number of other items. For example, ice cream, fresh fruit, whipped cream, or chocolate sauce are all a delightful pairing with this wonderful cake.

Zuccotto

This is a molded, cream filled dessert, said to be named for the domed ceiling in Florence, Italy's main cathedral. (The skull cap used by a cardinal is also called a zuccotto). The connection to things heavenly holds true with the presentation and incredibly rich taste of this dessert.

Shopping List

Nonstick cooking spray, or shortening

Plastic wrap

One pound cake (buy it or bake it, see recipe page 98)

$\frac{1}{2}$ cup of brandy

6-ozs. bitter sweet chocolate, chopped

2 cups heavy cream, well chilled (right from the fridge will do)

$\frac{1}{4}$ cup confectioner's sugar

$\frac{1}{2}$ tsp pure almond extract

$\frac{1}{2}$ cup toasted almond slices, chopped or coarsely crumbled

Unsweetened cocoa powder for dusting

Preparation

1. Start by spraying or lightly greasing a $1\frac{1}{2}$ quart bowl. (Hint: if you don't have a $1\frac{1}{2}$ quart bowl, get a bowl the nearest size larger, pour in $1\frac{1}{2}$ quarts of water and mark the side. There is your fill line). Now fully line the bowl with plastic wrap, leaving enough extra to wrap back over the bowl later.

2. Now for the pound cake. Trim any hard crust, and then cut the cake into about $\frac{1}{3}$ inch slices. Then make a diagonal cut into each slice, making two triangles.

3. Line the bowl, on top of the plastic wrap, with the pound cake slices, fitting them into a tight pattern, starting at the bottom and center of the bowl and extending up the sides, reserving some of the triangles for the bottom layer (top of the mold). Leave enough room at the top to place the final layer of triangles.

4. Lightly brush the triangles lining the bowl with brandy. Brush the reserved triangles on one side.

5. Now for the first filling.

    a. Using a double boiler, or a large metal bowl set over a sauce pan of simmering water, stir in the chocolate and let it melt, then set aside to cool to room temperature.

    b. Using another large mixing bowl, beat one cup of the heavy cream until it is thick and fluffy.

    c. Fold the whipped cream into the chocolate, in 3 parts as follows. First, fold $\frac{1}{4}$ of the whipped cream into the chocolate. Now fold $\frac{1}{2}$ of the remaining whipped cream into the chocolate mixture. Now fold in the remaining whipped cream.

6. Spoon the chocolate mixture into the pound cake mold, lining the bottom and sides, while leaving a hole in the middle

7. The second filling:

    a. Make sure the beaters in your mixer are clean. Using another large mixing bowl, beat the remaining one cup of heavy whipping cream, the confectioner's sugar, and the almond extract until you get firm peaks to form.

    b. Fold in the almonds.

8. Spoon second filling into the center of the hole created in the chocolate filling.

9. Take the reserved triangle slices of pound cake and piece them together for the base of the dessert, remembering to face the brandied sides of each piece into the interior of the dessert.

10. Cover the mold with the plastic wrap and refrigerate for at least four hours.

Serving: Invert the mold onto a serving platter and dust with the cocoa powder. For a little additional elegance, add line of whipped cream around the base of the Zuccotto. Heavenly.

Grasshopper Pie

I was familiar with Grasshopper Pie as an ice cream dessert...tasted great...turned to soup on warm summer evenings on the porch. This pie harkens back to an earlier time when chiffon fillings were in favor.

Shopping List

20 double stuffed Mint 'n Cream Oreo Cookies (or mix regular and mint flavored Oreos if you prefer a less pronounced mint taste)

3 Tbls of unsalted butter, melted and cooled

3 large egg yolks at room temperature

1 envelope of unflavored gelatin

$\frac{1}{2}$ cup granulated sugar

2 cups of heavy whipping cream

Pinch of salt (table salt, not a coarser grind)

$\frac{1}{4}$ cup green crème de menthe (green for the color of the finished filling)

$\frac{1}{4}$ cup white (clear) crème de cacao

Preparation

1. For the crust: start by crumbling the cookies into a food processor or blender, and pulse into a fine crumb. Or, crumble onto a sheet of waxed paper, cover with a second sheet of waxed paper, take a rolling pin and pound and roll into a fine crumb. Transfer this into a mixing bowl and drizzle in the melted butter. Mix well by hand or by using a whisk. Transfer this into a 9-inch pie plate, pressing the mixture evenly across the bottom and around the sides. The pie crust now needs to be refrigerated for about 20 minutes, or until the crust is firm to the touch.

2. Preheat oven to 350 degrees Fahrenheit, put piecrust on center rack in the oven, and bake for 8 to 10 minutes. Remove from the oven and cool on a wire rack.

3. For the filling: in a medium bowl, beat the egg yolks.

4. Combine the gelatin, sugar, $\frac{1}{2}$ cup of heavy cream, and salt in a medium saucepan and let it rest until the gelatin softens (about 5 minutes).

5. Cook over medium heat until the gelatin dissolves and the mixture is hot, but not boiling.

6. Whisking the egg yolks vigorously, slowly, SLOWLY, incorporate the gelatin mixture into the yolks (if you add the hot liquid too quickly, or whisk too slowly, you will scramble the yolks).

7. Return the mixture to the saucepan, and add heat, stirring constantly, until slightly thickened (about 2 minutes over medium heat).

8. Remove mixture from the heat and add the crème de menthe and crème de cacao. Pour this mixture into a clean bowl and refrigerate, stirring occasionally, until the mixture is wobbly but not set (20-25 minutes).

9. Take the remaining $1\frac{1}{2}$ cups of heavy cream and beat until stiff peaks form (don't overdo this, it makes a difference).

10. Retrieve the gelatin mixture from the refrigerator. Whisk 1 cup of the whipped cream into the mixture until completely incorporated. Take a spatula and gently fold the gelatin mixture into the remaining whipped cream until no white streaks are visible. Now use the spatula to scrape the mixture into your pie crust, smoothing the top. Refrigerate for at least 6 hours or overnight.

Serving: Serve with a bit of shaved chocolate on each piece, or a drizzle of chocolate syrup on top and around the plate, smile, and accept your marriage proposals.

Almond Puff Pies

I am normally a "from scratch" guy when it comes to my desserts. Not with puff pastry. Here I heartily recommend you buy the stuff pre-made.

Shopping List

1 pound of puff pastry (defrosted)

Confectioner's sugar for dusting

2 ½ Tbls (⅓ stick) of unsalted butter melted

2 ½ cups of ground almonds

1 ¼ cups of superfine sugar (you can make your own with a coffee grinder and regular granulated sugar)

3 Tbls of orange blossom water

Preparation

1. Divide the block of puff pastry into 4 blocks. Roll each pastry block out as thinly as possible, dusting your rolling pin and work surface with flour, turning the pastry and dusting each side in turn. Work the pastry out until you can cut 6 rounds with a 4-inch pastry cutter (or cut out a 4-inch circle of cardboard, use a bowl or glass with a 4-inch diameter, trace around it and cut with a paring knife). You will now have 24 little circlets. Put these circlets in a pile and wrap with plastic wrap. Refrigerate.

2. For the filling: combine the ground almonds, superfine sugar and orange blossom water and turn them into a paste. A food processor helps here.

3. Assemble. Take one of the puff circlets and put about one Tbls of the mixture into the center of the round. Fold the edges over forming a half moon shape and either pinch the edges together or use the tines of a fork to seal them. It goes much better if you moisten the edges with a little water on a finger.

4. Pre-heat your oven to a temperature of 400 degrees. Now line the bottom of a half sheet or baking tray with foil and arrange your pies on the tray. Brush each one with the melted butter. Pop them in the oven for about 15 minutes, or until the pastry has puffed and is a light golden brown.

5. Let them cool, and then dust with the confectioners' sugar before serving. If making in advance, dust just prior to serving.

Bear Comes to Visit and Brings Tim, Our Wine Specialist

Bear, a black Chow and the best dog in the world, is an annual guest at Sunny Shores and allows her family, Tim and Jeri Richardson, to accompany her on her vacation. Bear is very friendly with Luna and Bella (our cats) and any dog smaller than herself. She especially likes Tippy, the Reids' dog from next door who visits daily for brunch with Bella and Luna. Anyway, Tim is our resident wine expert and we all, including Bear, do the wine tours of northern Michigan each summer to taste and buy local wines for our dinners, doing our best to remain on our $10 per bottle budget. Tim admits that he started drinking vintage clarets when he was ten years old supplied by his uncle Humphrey (who was also a close friend of mine) when he lived in England with his parents.

I've had many wonderful dinners at their home. Jeri is a great cook, and Tim will ask her what we're having for dinner, then go to his extensive wine rack and contemplate on his selection for the evening's repast. It's a great experience to dine with Tim and Jeri and benefit from his knowledge. Tim's wine recommendations appear at the end of each menu and are summarized on the following pages.

Consolidated Wine Suggestions

All the wine suggestions and comments are courtesy of Tim Richardson of Houston, Texas. Tim is well known for his knowledge of wine, and he and his wife Jeri are regular guests at Sunny Shores. All of Tim's suggestions are for a general type of wine and not a specific label. He did not name any specific wines because it is likely that what is available in Houston may be unobtainable in Michigan. Following is a summary of all of Tim's suggestions that are also included at the end of each corresponding menu.

Menu I:

Recommend: Gigondas (French, from the Rhone valley).

Alternatives: Cotes-du-Rhone, Chateauneuf-du-Pape, American Syrah

Menu II:

Recommend: Austrian Riesling or Alsace Pinot Blanc

Alternatives: There are nice domestic counterparts, ask your local wine store owner

Menu III:

Recommend: Chianti

Alternatives: other North Italian reds (e.g. Barbera, Valpolicella), red Saumur or Chinon (French), Beaujolais (e.g. Brouilly). American table wine

Local possibility: Michigan Cabernet Franc

Menu IV:

Recommend: A good full-bodied Bordeaux or American Claret

Alternatives: A good Cabernet Sauvignon would also go nicely with lamb

Menu V:

Recommend: French Burgundy

Alternatives: American Pinot Noir

(Tim's comment: this was a tough one because you can probably use just about any red wine for the coq au vin – Merlot, Cabernet Sauvignon etc. – in fact white wine is not unheard of either. Traditionally, French burgundy is used, but it tends to be expensive! One option is to cook with a less expensive pinot noir and drink the burgundy.)

Menu VI:

  Recommend: Cahors (French)

  Alternatives: Argentine or Chilean malbec, American Zinfandel

(Comment: Cahors is not too easy to find, but Malbecs are. Beef Stroganoff definitely calls for a robust red wine. This is not going to go well with the salad, so you might hold off serving it until the main course. Tomatoes are very hard to match with wine!)

Menu VII:

  Recommend: Austrian Riesling or Gruner Veltliner

  Alternatives: NZ or American Sauvignon Blanc, Entre-Deux-Mers (white Bordeaux)

  Local possibility: Michigan Riesling

  If you prefer red: Valpolicella

Menu VIII:

  Recommend: Rioja (Spanish)

  Alternatives: Minervois (Southern France), Australian Shiraz

  If you prefer white: Pinot Grigio (recommended for the marinade), American Viognier

Menu IX:

  Recommend: Bairrada (Portuguese). For the gravlax, shots of ice-cold aquavit or vodka!

  Alternatives: Ribera del Duero (Spanish), Dao (Portuguese), Nemea (Greek),French Bordeaux

  If you prefer white: French Burgundy, non-oaky American Chardonnay

Menu X:

  Recommend: Strongly recommends red Bordeaux (2005 was a good year)

  Alternatives: American or Australian Cabernet Sauvignon

Index of Recipes

Appetizers

Main Courses

Main Course Side Dishes

Desserts

Crystal Lake Beach

The beach in front of our little summer cottage on Crystal Lake has been one of my favorite places since I was a child. It's fairly small with maybe room for six beach chairs. In the summer, the sand is always warm and you can dig your toes down several inches before reaching the hard, damp sand. As you sit on the beach and look out over the lake, you can see the sandy bottom of the lake along with perch minnows, snails, and the occasional crawfish. On a really calm day you can even see the little trails the snails leave in the sand as they move across the bottom. Several feet further out, the lake deepens and the color of the water changes to a royal blue, then almost navy out towards the middle of the lake. The sun makes the top of the water sparkle and twinkle like sparklers on the Fourth of July. The sound of the water splashing against the shore is always there, even when the occasional boat goes by or the sounds of kids playing drift down the beach. There is an abundance of wildflowers between the cottage and the beach and you can usually catch their fragrance on the breeze mixing with the fragrance of the pine trees in the woods behind the house. When I really listen, I can hear the buzz of the bumblebees in the wildflower patches blending with the rustling of the birch trees. And, if I am really still, I can hear my grandmother calling me to come in off the beach for dinner.